THE WILLI
SERVANT

A history
of electricity
in the home

by
Anthony Byers

UNDERSTANDING ELECTRICITY
Educational Service

Published by The Electricity Council,
30 Millbank, London SW1P 4RD

Acknowledgements: Bob Gordon of the Milne Museum, Brian Bowers of the Science Museum, Gwen Conacher, Dick Hancock and Jenny Webb of the Electricity Council and the British manufacturers of electrical appliances for their advice and help. The help of the National Trust, the Milne Museum at Tonbridge and the Science Museum are also acknowledged for obtaining many of the photographs.

First published in 1981 to mark the centenary of public electricity supply under the title CENTENARY OF SERVICE, this new edition has been revised and updated.

ISBN 0-85188-086-X

Designed by GBW Design Ltd.
Printed by Camgate Litho Ltd.

CONTENTS

The Willing Servants *(first published under the title Centenary of Service)* is produced by the Understanding Electricity educational information service sponsored by the electricity supply industries in the United Kingdom and the Republic of Ireland and by the United Kingdom Atomic Energy Authority. Its aim is to improve the knowledge of young people about basic electrical principles and their practical applications. Information is provided on the generation and transmission of electricity as well as background material on the use of electricity in commerce, agriculture, horticulture, industry and the home.

ONCE UPON A TIME

Previous page: Among the first of the electricity generating stations were Brighton (1882) above, and Deptford (1889) below.

Opposite page: Street lighting in Godalming and a sketch of the water mill from The Graphic, November 12, 1881.

When the townspeople of Godalming saw their streets light up one September evening in 1881 they never guessed they were making history. The lamps were lit by electricity and the power came from a generator connected to a waterwheel – the first public supply of electricity from a generating station.

There was so little sense of history in the occasion that nobody knows for certain the exact date of the switch-on that gave a supply for lighting and for private customers. The Town Council of this small market town in Surrey, 37 miles from London, simply recorded on 1st October 1881 that the annual contract for electricity was costing £95, a saving of £15 a year compared with the cost of gas lighting!

In the hundred years since that switch was operated on the generator in the watermill on the River Wey, electricity has changed the civilised world. Without electricity the mechanisation of the home, with all the time and labour saving benefits, would not have occurred. Life today is totally dependent on it.

Think of the electrical appliances that would not exist if there were no electricity. Count the number of pieces of electrical equipment and lights you have in the home and do not be surprised if you soon reach one hundred. Even the telephone needs electricity and a great many toys and games work from electric batteries.

Electricity is a form of energy (the power to do work) that is produced from other forms of energy – such as mechanical rotation or chemical reaction. Its advantage over all other types of energy is its instant convenience. It is available at the flick of a switch and adaptable to a far wider range of uses than the other kinds of energy. It is very clean in use, there is no smell or smoke, and it is very easy to regulate electrical appliances automatically by thermostats, time switches and electronic controls such as those with the micro-chip.

At the touch of a switch, pure power is available through a socket on the wall from a power station many, many miles away. Instantly, it removes the muscular effort from all sorts of tasks like drilling a hole or mixing a cake. It will also provide good lighting; it will give more leisure and comfort and help to feed you. It will then entertain you with sound and vision right in your

THE TOWN OF GODALMING ILLUMINATED BY THE ELECTRIC LIGHT

living room. Electricity is man's most remarkable phenomenon and his most willing servant.

Beginning of electricity

Although the electricity supply industry is one hundred years old, the history of electricity is much older. Thousands of years before electricity's behaviour was accurately explained and its powers harnessed to man's use, magnetism was well known. The electro-magnetic properties of lodestone – a variety of iron oxide called magnetite – were so highly prized that if any sailor in the Middle Ages was caught tampering with a ship's lodestone, "he shall, if his life be spared, be punished by having the hand which he most uses, fastened by a dagger or knife thrust through it, to the mast or principal timber of the ship".

As magnetite seeks to line itself in a northerly direction everywhere on earth, the lodestone was used to magnetise the compass needles used by sailors to find their way across uncharted seas. Without it a ship would be virtually lost, able to navigate only by the sun and the stars.

Dr William Gilbert, physician to Queen Elizabeth 1 in 1600, carried out experiments on lodestone magnetism. He was the first to use the word electricity which he derived from the Greek word *elektron,* meaning amber. For when amber is rubbed vigorously it attracts small particles of dust – the effect we call static electricity.

For the next 150 years, 'electricity' attracted the curiosity of scientists. Some even suggested that it could be used to solve the most popular scientific problem of the age – a means of turning base metal into gold.

Then in 1746, Pieter van Musschenbroek, a professor at Leyden University, discovered by accident that electricity could be stored in what became known as the Leyden Jar. This was a water filled glass jar encircled by a metal band, electricity being stored in the glass between the metal and the water.

Musschenbroek also discovered the dangerous effect of 'electric shock'. An accidental electric shock prostrated him for two days and frightened him so much that he said he "would not take another for the Kingdom of France".

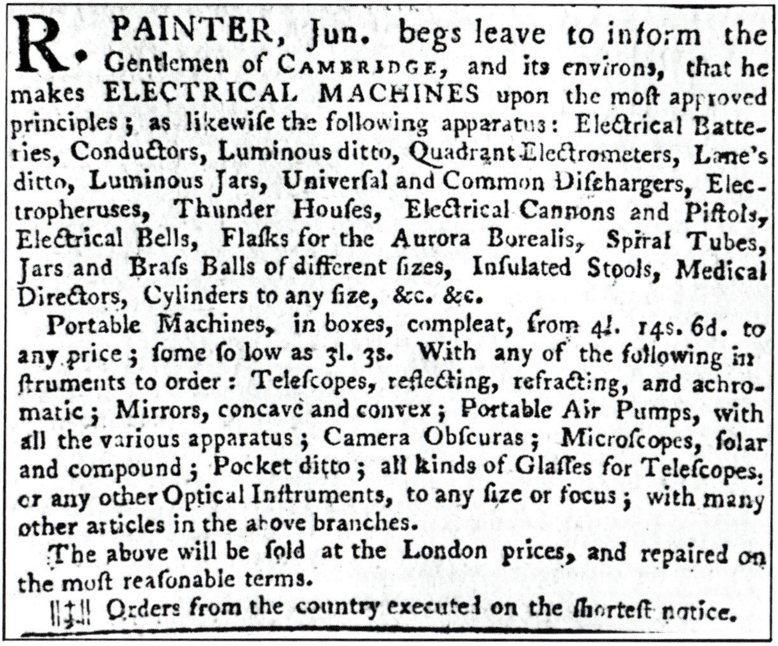

R. PAINTER, Jun. begs leave to inform the Gentlemen of CAMBRIDGE, and its environs, that he makes ELECTRICAL MACHINES upon the moſt approved principles; as likewiſe the following apparatus: Electrical Batteries, Conductors, Luminous ditto, Quadrant Electrometers, Lane's ditto, Luminous Jars, Univerſal and Common Diſchargers, Electropheruses, Thunder Houſes, Electrical Cannons and Piſtols, Electrical Bells, Flaſks for the Aurora Borealis, Spiral Tubes, Jars and Braſs Balls of different ſizes, Inſulated Stools, Medical Directors, Cylinders to any ſize, &c. &c.

Portable Machines, in boxes, compleat, from 4l. 14s. 6d. to any price; ſome ſo low as 3l. 3s. With any of the following inſtruments to order: Teleſcopes, reflecting, refracting, and achromatic; Mirrors, concave and convex; Portable Air Pumps, with all the various apparatus; Camera Obſcuras; Microſcopes, ſolar and compound; Pocket ditto; all kinds of Glaſſes for Teleſcopes, or any other Optical Inſtruments, to any ſize or focus; with many other articles in the above branches.

The above will be ſold at the London prices, and repaired on the moſt reaſonable terms.

‖‡‖ Orders from the country executed on the ſhorteſt notice.

Scientific curiosity encouraged experiment and invention. This advertisement appeared in The Cambridge Chronicle, November 23, 1786.

Electricity for cooking

Benjamin Franklin, in America in the following year also carried out an electrical experiment which very nearly killed him. He and his son never realised that they might get electrocuted when they sent up a kite during a thunderstorm. They were simply trying to prove that lightning is electrical in nature. An electric spark jumped from a metal key tied to the end of the string to charge a Leyden Jar and from this Franklin concluded that electricity consisted of "a kind of fluid". His curiosity aroused, he conducted further experiments and he was the first person to use electricity for cooking. After a picnic he wrote "I killed a turkey by the electric spark and roasted it by an electric jack before a fire kindled by the electric bottle".

Modern atomic theory has superseded Franklin's fluid theory of electricity. Today, the generation of an electrical charge by friction can be explained by the structure of atoms. But back in the eighteenth century all the experimenters knew was that electricity did not appear to do anything, or even exist, until it had somewhere to go. They observed that it usually only wanted to find a path straight to earth. Today, we know that when you plug in or switch on electricity, you complete a circuit: the current passes through the electrical appliance, providing motive power, heat or light, and then – its work done – returns to the generator.

Opposite page: The Electrical Development Association produced persuasive publicity to encourage wider use of electricity.

In 1821 Michael Faraday demonstrated that a wire connected to a battery would rotate around the fixed magnet and, in a similar fashion, it could be arranged so that the magnet would rotate around a wire. This conversion of electricity into mechanical work was the first electric motor. Ten years later in 1831 he demonstrated the reverse – that electricity could be induced into a conductor by a changing magnetic field.

It was to take another 50 years before Faraday's discoveries had been sufficiently developed to enable dynamo-electric generators to be built that were capable of supplying a public supply of electricity on a commercial basis. A further thirty years passed before generated electricity was available at a price that people could afford. Even in 1910 only about 2% of households were wired for electricity.

The first steam power station opened in London (Holborn) on 12th January 1882 and six weeks later Brighton power station provided the first permanent public supply of electricity.

Two other power stations opened later that year, at Hastings and Eastbourne, and cables were laid in the streets with the consent of the local authority. Almost at the same time Parliament passed the Electric Lighting Act which, among other regulations, gave the first statutory right for a person near to a power station to demand a supply of electricity for his factory or his home.

By 1914 there were enough power stations and a growing number of customers to make electricity relatively cheap although, until the National Grid was established in 1926, there were big differences in the prices charged between the different companies.

In 1919 the British Electrical Development Association (soon simply known as EDA) was formed to promote the wide use of electricity. It used all the popular means – including poetry – to promote the sales of electrical appliances and lighting on behalf of the growing number of electrical companies and supply

The Rúbaiyát of the Electric House.

Awake: The Time-switch by the warm Bed's Side
Has boiled your Kettle ere the Cock has Cried:
And Lo: The Tea is ready, fill the Cup,
And chuckle as the Rain pours down outside.

Come, press the Switch, and as the radiant Glow
Foretells the Sparkling Water's warming Flow,
Pity those Neighbours who, 'fore Sticks and Coal,
Kneel on their Hearths and wheezing Bellows Blow.

I always think that nothing tastes so sweet
As juicy, cooked-electrically Meat,
That every Meal prepared in selfsame way
Incites each jaded Mortal more to eat.

Ah, make the most of where ye have to stay
As too brief Sojourners in Life's short Way,
While in that Chamber where your Guests repose
Lie those who bless your Name from Dusk to Day:

Ah, use the Juice :—and let the Mains provide
Such Warmth as never with Cold Ashes died,
And to the Scrap Heap of Oblivion fling
The Greedy Range with blackened Jaws set wide.

For, since my House has been Electrified,
Dirt and Discomfort have for ever died,
And with them past Regrets and future Fears,
While Light hath taken Beauty for his Bride.

Spring Cleanliness Every Day

ELECTRICITY
"SAVES MORE THAN IT COSTS"

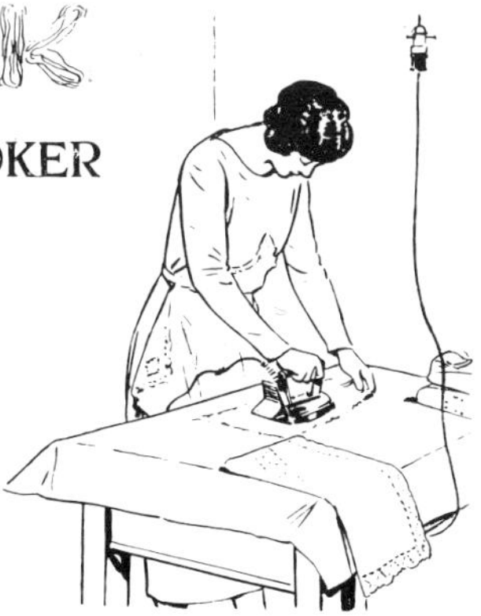

undertakings.

By 1925 the national average price of electricity had come down – especially for use other than lighting – and Victor Dale, the Manager of EDA, was writing in the Financial Times: "Conversion to electric methods in established populous areas will assist more than anything else to mitigate the smoke evil and progressively reduce the air-polluting emissions from domestic chimneys. Longer hours of "better sunshine" will be one only of the first results accruing from more or less complete domestic electrification in this country – the contention will not be lost on those who recollect the cleanness of the atmosphere in the Metropolis during the protracted miners' strike of 1923."

Cleaner air, convenience, time and labour saving and its ability to perform tasks beyond the powers of any other form of energy, these were the benefits that impressed the public and by 1939 almost three quarters of the homes in the United Kingdom had electricity laid on.

With the celebration of the centenary, the United Kingdom can boast the largest electricity supply organisation in the world. It continues to be an innovator in forms of generation such as nuclear power and pumped storage; in transmission, like the unified grid system which reduces the risk of prolonged breakdown by switching power from one area to another.

The Electricity Boards, as well as assuring a reliable supply, also operate a nationwide chain of retail shops that offer free advice as well as appliances tested for safety, and control a service organisation that – for electricity supply – is there, seven days a week and twenty-four hours a day.

In 1881 the Godalming generating station employed about five people; in 1947, when the electricity supply industry came under public ownership, there were 147,000 employees and eleven million customers in England and Wales. Today, the number of employees is almost 160,000 and there are more than twenty million customers supplied from 127 generating stations – coal, oil, water, gas and nuclear power.

LET THERE BE LIGHT

THE INTRODUCTION OF THE ELECTRIC LIGHT, ETC., INTO PRIVATE HOUSES.

1. Warning to people who wear sham jewellery, if an unprotected wire happens to touch a necklet, &c.; for instance, the above might possibly happen. 2. "Please, ma'am, the man 's called with the storage force—will you have it in the cask or bottle?" 3. Jones thinks the light much too strong. 4. Master Harry takes Tommy to show him their new battery. 5. Quadrille of the future in a room overcharged with an escape of electricity. 6. Curious accident by the careless use of an electric pipe-lighter. 7. Portraits of gentlemen who have had the electric fluid in their houses for a few years. 8. The Christmas galvanic batter(y)-pudding, electric currants, &c.

The story of electric lighting

Previous page: Electricity was a popular source of humour in the 1890s when it began to be widely used for lighting homes.

It is difficult to imagine what everyday life was like before there was electric lighting. Huge crowds gathered in 1848 to see demonstrations of electric arc lighting from batteries and, while it was reported as "a great wonder" it also aroused unfounded fears not unlike some of those expressed today about scientific development. "Magnetism is an unnatural force in nature", wrote one critic. Another described electricity as "a phenomenon of the devil", and the subject attracted music hall jokes and satirical cartoons in popular journals.

"What need we with light, the Lord hath given us the dark to rest", said a clergyman preaching on the biblical text: "the night cometh when no man can work" (John X: 14). For there were even those who disapproved of oil and gas lamps which, along with candles and wax tapers, remained the popular sources of artificial lighting until towards the end of the nineteenth century.

By 1825 almost half a million gas lamps had been installed in the two hundred miles of London streets. This was the result of the Lord Mayor of London urging for better lighting: "great numbers of evilly disposed persons armed with bludgeons, pistols, cutlasses and other dangerous weapons infest not only the private lanes and passages, but likewise the public streets and places of public concourse."

Lacking proper street lighting most of those who lived in the cities and towns stayed at home at night or took advantage of a full moon to "venture abroad", or hired "link boys" with smoking torches to accompany them. "So dark was the lane", wrote Parson Woodforde in his diary in 1787, "that I fell down in mud three times before I reached my gate much discomforted."

There were many who believed that had the East End streets been better lighted, the nineteenth century Jack the Ripper would have been caught and perhaps Charles Dickens might have written very different books. Certainly smoke and heat from burning lights, together with the chimneys, contributed to London's 'pea soup' fogs. Sir Frederick French in 1839 observed that candle and oil lighting was unhealthy: "one wax candle consumes as much oxygen as two men."

Electric lighting was to help change all that. After the 1846 demonstrations of arc lighting, a surge of electrical invention and application began but, lacking a proper form of electrical generation, few of the methods proved immediately practical.

Public lighting

In 1878 the Gaiety Theatre in London and the Bramall Lane ground of the Sheffield Football Club were lit by arc lamps for a short time. The following year Blackpool put on the first of their famous seaside illuminations. Two years later a mixture of arc and incandescent filament lamps were installed to light the streets of Godalming in Surrey, Norwich in Norfolk and Chesterfield in Derbyshire, and filament lamps were used to light the Savoy Theatre and the House of Commons.

Despite these successes a committee reported: "We are quite satisfied that the electric light can never be applied indoors without production of an offensive smell which undoubtedly causes headaches, and in its naked state it can never be used in rooms of even large size without damage to sight." The gas lighting companies and their shareholders breathed a sigh of relief.

Although their relief was to be short lived, there was a certain truth to the committee's statement. Arc lamps gave off a very strong white light when electric current or a spark was passed between carbon rods but often this also produced both smoke and an unpleasant smell. A better, cleaner method was to pass a current through a wire which, as it heated, glowed and gave off visible light. The problem was to find a filament wire which would reach a high temperature without melting.

In 1878 (the same year as the committee's report) Sir Joseph Swan experimented with a carbon filament. A carbon filament had an extremely high melting point and gave a good light but it rapidly burnt away in air. He then had the idea of placing the filament inside a glass bulb from which most of the air had been removed and the bulb sealed. This was the first practical filament lamp and in 1880 Swan installed some in his home at Low Fell, Gateshead. This was the first house in the world to be lighted by electricity using these lamps. Later that year Sir William Armstrong built the world's first hydro electric installation to provide electricity to light his picture gallery at Cragside,

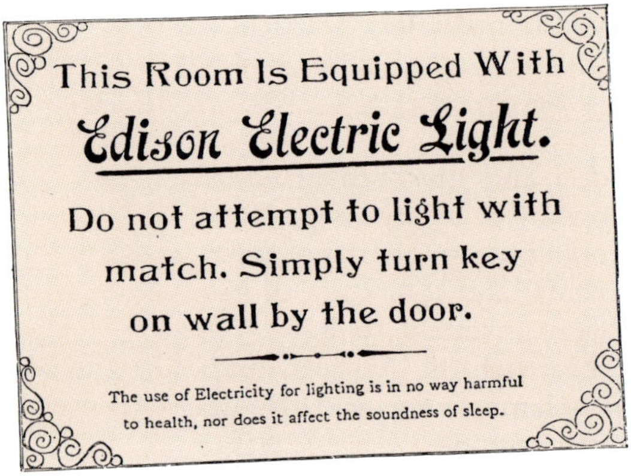

Northumberland (now a National Trust property) using Swan's lamps.

Independently, in America, Thomas Edison had come up with a similar solution and in 1883 he combined his ideas with Swan's to form the Edison & Swan Electric Light Co. Ltd., although already there were rivals making lamps in all sorts of shapes and patterns.

Electric lighting had arrived. It proved, though, quite hard at first to convince people that an electric lamp did not have to be lit by a match. Special notices had to be printed for hotels and public rooms.

Opposite page: A century of progress in lamp design beginning with Swan's filament glass bulb and leading to the latest miniature fluorescents that fit into the conventional lampholder.

By 1906 tungsten was being used for the filament instead of carbon. In 1913 an inert gas – nitrogen and then argon – was put into the glass bulb which enabled the coiled filament to become even hotter so it gave off more light. The problem (one still to be satisfactorily solved) was that the filament lamp proved to be better at heating than lighting; ninety per cent of the electric current being turned directly into heat and only ten per cent used for lighting. (see also Page 15).

Edison in 1896 tried to overcome this basic drawback of the filament by passing current not through a metal filament but through a glass tube with a coating that gave off light – "fluoresced" – but his early experiments ended in failure. It needed another forty years of research by others before, in 1936, an efficient fluorescent lamp was produced – the prototype of the modern fluorescent tube that is capable of giving five or more times as much light for the same consumption as the filament lamp and has fifteen times its life.

Research also went into improving the arc (discharge) lamp that had been the first successful form of electric lighting. In 1901 a lamp filled with mercury vapour proved that a great amount of useful light could be obtained from a small amount of current. One drawback was that the light was blue and created a "ghostly

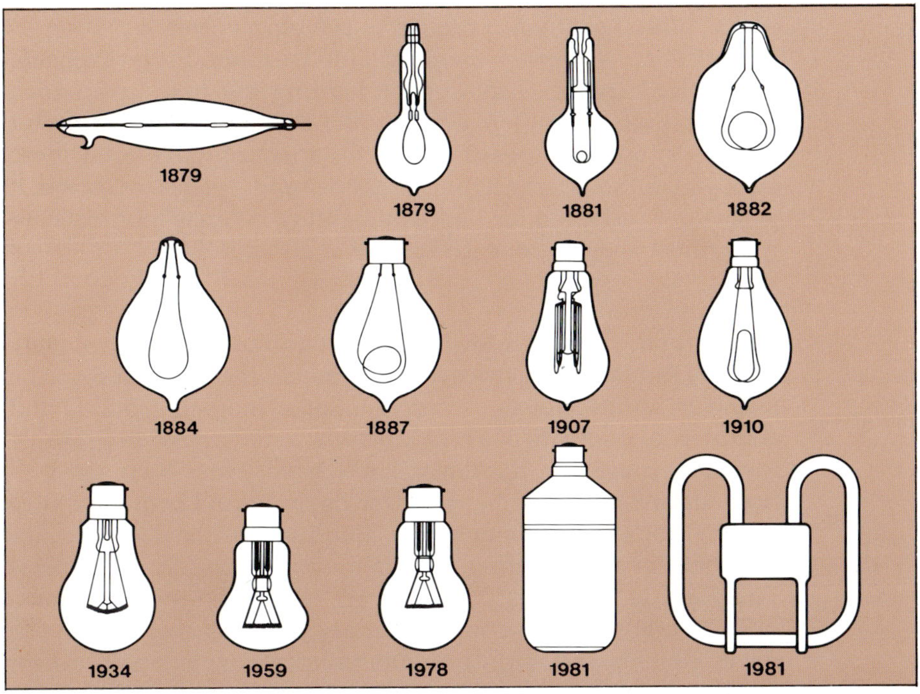
1879
1879
1881
1882
1884
1887
1907
1910
1934
1959
1978
1981
1981

effect" although it was possible to see objects clearly.

By 1930 a *high pressure* mercury lamp was found to be a reliable and a not expensive answer for lighting the new urban road systems that were then being built. By 1935 a version using sodium at a lower pressure than the mercury gave even more light and, although the light was deep orange/yellow in colour, it was widely adopted for highway lighting because motorists are not critical about colour if visibility is good.

Modern lighting

Opposite page: Concealed, controllable lighting in the modern home contrasts with the fittings offered in Harrods Catalogue in 1929, many adapted from gas lamps.

Today, both high and low pressure sodium lamps are widely used by industry while variations of the discharge lamp are to be found in shops, hotels, railway stations, football grounds and commercial premises of every kind where they provide a reliable low-cost source of lighting. Some have even been used in horticulture to supplement winter daylight and provide out of season crops. They are not to be found in the home as yet since the high level of lighting output they are capable of giving is rarely needed. Fluorescent lamps are usually far more suitable.

The outbreak of war in 1939 brought the blackout. Lighting developments and improvements came almost to a halt, except for the specialised wartime needs such as landing lights for airfields.

When the war was ended it was fluorescent tubes that were to become the most popular form of lighting. One thousand million tubes are made every year throughout the world and fluorescent lighting now accounts for around 80% of the world's artificial light. Fluorescents have even moved into the home. Slim tubes are made to light shelves and alcoves; short tubes are made for bathrooms, linked with a special socket for electric shavers; and there are even circular tubes for ceiling lighting. The latest development is also small enough to fit into a conventional lampholder.

As for the filament lamp ("lamp" is the correct name, rather than "bulb", and lighting fittings are now called "luminaires") improvements have been made to lengthen its life and increase its performance. One development to improve the light output was to wind the filament into a tight, tiny double coil (stretched out it would be 115 cm long (4 ft) in a 100 Watt lamp). Lamps of

ELECTRICAL DEPARTMENT
Every Conceivable Electrical Lighting Fitting is Available at Harrods
WALL BRACKET
TWO-LIGHT SLIDING PENDANT
MODERN ONE-LIGHT PANEL BRACKET
FLEXIBLE READING LAMP
CEILING LIGHT
SHELL CRAFT
PENDANT
SHELL CRAFT
ALL PRICES ARE SUBJECT TO MARKET FLUCTUATIONS
HARRODS LTD
LONDON S W 1

this type, which first appeared in 1938, are usually called "coiled-coil".

An even more remarkable development came in 1961 with the tungsten halogen filament lamp – originally called the quartz iodine lamp. Neat and compact, more than fifty per cent brighter and lasting two to three times longer than other filament lamps, it first came into use as a tiny but immensely powerful light source for ciné projectors. Now the narrow, glass phial lamps are used for outdoor floodlighting, indoor display lighting and car headlamps.

In the early days of electric lighting in the home, the electric lamp was placed in the centre of the ceiling or against a wall, taking the place of the gas mantle. Now, with spotlights, downlights and dimmers as well as lights for general illumination, home lighting has become as much a part of decoration as the wall coverings and furnishings.

Lighting technology is not standing still. A new type of discharge lamp was invented back in 1947 that had a brightness equal to the sun and an application for the Xenon lamp has been in lighthouses. One installed in a lighthouse in New Zealand can be seen twenty miles away in daylight.

Football grounds are lighted today by 1000 Watt lamps that measure only 200 mm (8 in) in diameter. These are the sealed beam iodine lamps and lighting technology of this kind is now giving more light from smaller sources with a longer life.

Possibly the most surprising development of all is the use of light itself as an incredibly powerful energy source. The laser, researched by Theo Maiman in America in 1960, is an intense, narrow beam of light, so concentrated that a beam 1 cm in diameter at its source spreads to a few kilometres when it reaches the moon 250,000 miles away.

Among the most promising uses of the laser (Light Amplification by Simulated Emission of Radiation) is for delicate welding, including fixing the retina in the human eye, and for holography – producing pictures in the form of a three dimensional image.

In a little over one hundred years lighting – electricity's first contribution to human betterment, welfare and comfort – has come a long, long way.

HEARTH TO HOB

The story of electric cooking

The first iron cooking stove was made in China somewhere between 100 – 200 A.D. but it was to take over seventeen hundred years before anything like it appeared in Britain. All cooking was done over an open hearth fire or in a brick oven.

Previous page: An early EDA advertisement for electric cooking.

The fuel for cooking was wood or charcoal although, from the beginning of the eighteen hundreds, in the towns and in larger country homes, sea coal (so called because it was largely transported by sea and inland via the new canal system) was more frequently used as it burned longer and more evenly. Charcoal had been used for cooking since Roman times but it was considered unhealthy and, by 1800, there was already a shortage of the native timber from which it was derived, for the great forests like Sherwood and Dean had been cleared to create more land for growing food.

Most homes in the late eighteenth century had a hearth. Except in the wealthier houses, the hearth was in the living room where it served to heat the room and do the cooking. An iron basket normally held the fuel. This stopped the fire being clogged with ash while the draught from underneath made it burn better. Some also had an iron box that fitted beside or behind the grate and this was used for baking and roasting. It was this that encouraged the development of a stove capable of higher cooking temperatures and holding in the heat.

In 1802, George Bodley, an iron founder in Exeter, patented a closed top cooking stove. Made of cast iron, it had a small grate, an oven and a flat surface for heating pans. It was so successful that, in the following years, all sorts of "improved versions" appeared. By the end of the century, in all the rows of houses built for factory workers in the industrial towns and cities, every one had an iron grate, side oven and a hotplate that had been fitted into an open hearth and bricked in. Some even provided hot water and heating to other rooms and most were beautiful, decorative examples of the iron founder's art.

Such was the popularity of the iron stove that it was not so much the smoke from the factories and mills that created the grey grime and dark fog in the Victorian cities and towns, as the continuous outpouring from millions of small, low chimneys connected to stoves burning cheap coal. The atmosphere in towns and cities was far from healthy and lung and chest diseases were a major cause of early death.

Another disadvantage was that most stoves had to have the ash removed and be relit each morning. Also, the only way to clean cast iron was to "blacklead" – an unpleasant task which needed to be done regularly if it was to look clean and smart.

Gas, made from coal, was tested for cooking in 1812 but, since few homes had a kitchen, it was not thought practical. Most of the research was towards keeping the flame as cool as possible as it was used to give light not heat. Gas was also expensive compared with coal from the new mines opening in Scotland, the North East and Wales.

In 1824 a gas "grill" was designed and made in Liverpool and this became popular in hotel kitchens. As the heat was more easily controlled and it proved to be faster than cooking by heat from below, it encouraged the introduction of gas ranges in 1841. Even so it was not until well into the second half of the nineteenth century that a gas "stove" was available for homes in towns and cities where a cheap town gas supply had been provided for lighting.

Electric stoves

The possibility of using electricity for cooking was examined in 1885 but it was concluded that "the absence of a true flame renders it unsuitable." Fortunately, there were those who thought otherwise, recognising that it would be cleaner in use and, in 1891, electric cookers were demonstrated at an electrical exhibition at Crystal Palace.

The first practical electric cooker for the home was designed in Britain by H.F. Dowsing and marketed in 1893 by Crompton & Company of

Above: Electric hot plate from France 1900.

Below: An electric oven from the Crompton catalogue of 1899.

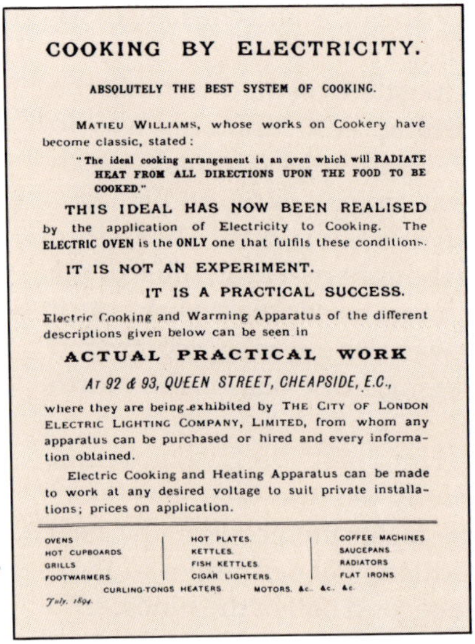

COOKING BY ELECTRICITY.

ABSOLUTELY THE BEST SYSTEM OF COOKING.

MATIEU WILLIAMS, whose works on Cookery have become classic, stated:

"The ideal cooking arrangement is an oven which will RADIATE HEAT FROM ALL DIRECTIONS UPON THE FOOD TO BE COOKED."

THIS IDEAL HAS NOW BEEN REALISED by the application of Electricity to Cooking. The **ELECTRIC OVEN** is the **ONLY** one that fulfils these conditions.

IT IS NOT AN EXPERIMENT.

IT IS A PRACTICAL SUCCESS.

Electric Cooking and Warming Apparatus of the different descriptions given below can be seen in

ACTUAL PRACTICAL WORK

AT 92 & 93, QUEEN STREET, CHEAPSIDE, E.C.,

where they are being exhibited by THE CITY OF LONDON ELECTRIC LIGHTING COMPANY, LIMITED, from whom any apparatus can be purchased or hired and every information obtained.

Electric Cooking and Heating Apparatus can be made to work at any desired voltage to suit private installations; prices on application.

OVENS	HOT PLATES	COFFEE MACHINES
HOT CUPBOARDS	KETTLES	SAUCEPANS
GRILLS	FISH KETTLES	RADIATORS
FOOTWARMERS	CIGAR LIGHTERS	FLAT IRONS

CURLING-TONGS HEATERS MOTORS, &c., &c., &c.

July, 1894.

One of the first advertisements for electric cooking (1894).

Opposite page: This 10 kW Carron cooker installed in a Croydon, Surrey, home in 1900 was in daily use until 1975.

Chelmsford (whose founder, Colonel Crompton, was one of the pioneers of electrical power for the home). The idea was soon copied by others even though it was said of electric stoves that "cakes baked by this apparatus have an indefinable electrical flavour"!

The first electric "stoves" were made of cast iron in designs almost indistinguishable from the gas cookers "as an unfamiliar appearance might alarm servants uneducated to this new force." This was a comment from Carron Ironfounders (who are still making electric cookers today) who also admitted that their stoves were regarded as more of a scientific novelty.

By 1894 the City of London Electric Lighting Company Limited were offering electricity at "four pence per unit" and on 15th June 1894, electric stoves were used by them for a promotional "all-electric banquet". This was the first public dinner cooked by electricity – six large ovens with hot-plates being used for 120 guests. The Company followed this up by issuing an advertising leaflet offering cookers for hire from seven shillings to twelve shillings a quarter, when a shilling represented something like £1 in today's buying values.

Everyone who attended the numerous cooking demonstrations, organised by the City of London Lighting Co Ltd, was impressed, although some feared that "the magnetic forces may enter the food with a deleterious effect upon the digestion". So wrote a correspondent in the popular journal, *John Bull.*

The controls for these early electric "stoves" were placed in a box on the wall nearby with a set of impressive looking brass switches. "The servants must be warned not to dowse water upon these switches no matter the provocation" was the instruction of one of the first customers to his cook. The servants

might well have been frightened as these cooker control boxes often gave off sparks, flashes and even a sinister humming.

The price of electricity came down as power stations were built in every city. Fears of any possible dangers soon faded as the many advantages were seen. "It is fairly clear," wrote Mr A.F. Berry in 1917, "that one ton of coal burned at the generating station of an electricity works suffices to do the cooking that ordinarily requires ten tons of coal in a private house."

Mr Berry was writing towards the end of the First World War and he was illustrating the use and economy of his Tricity electric cookers in munition workers' canteens and field kitchens.

It was this war that was to reduce the number of domestic servants from two and a quarter million in 1914 to less than a million in 1919. For several centuries domestic service had been the principal form of employment open to working women; now they could earn more money working in a factory and so post war housewives had to do their own cooking where previously they might have employed a cook. One thing was

Left to right:
Belling 'Modernette' cooker of 1919.
Falco cookers of 1914 and 1925.

immediately clear: housewives were not going to use the dirty troublesome coal range they had inflicted on their servants.

In 1919 Belling introduced the small "Modernette" cooker made of sheet metal, developed from a lightweight design created in the war years for cooking in submarines. It offered to a post war population, faced with low salaries and unemployment, a low cost, lightweight, simple, reliable cooker and the only thing preventing it from capturing popular appeal was that in the "Roaring Twenties" only about a fifth of the homes in Great Britain were connected to the main supply. The introduction of a "flat rate tariff" – one charge for lighting and one for cooking and heating – coupled with all sorts of low cost offers to have your house wired, began to open up the market and the demand for electric cookers grew.

In 1935 a Baby Belling cooker with an oven and small hob could be bought for under £4 and a small electric heating ring cost 19s.6d. (98p).

Most families hired their electric cooker from the electric company. Hiring was more common than outright purchase for both gas and electric cookers until about 1938 – a practice which, unfortunately, tended to discourage innovation. The models had to be robustly built and improvements which might have made existing models obsolete, and so unsuitable for rehiring, were largely ignored.

Among the new ideas whose application was delayed by this practice was the thermostat. This was capable of controlling the oven heat automatically but until 1938 a thermometer and a three heat switch were the only means of monitoring and

Left to right: Electric cooker manufacturers after 1945 strove to improve performance and design. A cooker made in aluminium (1945) and a new design with the oven above the hob and storage space beneath (1955) both by English Electric. One of the first of the waist high ovens (1956) made by 'English Rose'. A double width cooker (1953) and a popular model of 1958 with a viewing window for the oven, both by Creda.

adjusting the oven temperature. The cook had constantly to alter the switch and time the cooking carefully.

Some ovens now had a frameless, glass inner door and, by 1939, the solid hotplates on the hob had been improved so they heated up and cooled down more quickly. They were more easily controllable, too, and it was no longer necessary to follow a tip used, up to that time, of placing a small coin between the boiling plate and the pan if you wanted to "simmer" food.

The oven now had open wire elements set behind removable panels and, by 1940, when production of all domestic appliances ceased, the basic design of the electric cooker with hob over a grill chamber and an oven had been established.

The first of the post war cookers was a copy of a 1939 design, although new materials were being tested. The English Electric Company in 1945 used their wartime skills in building aircraft to make a cooker in aluminium "to avoid the bottleneck in iron castings and help the National Housing Drive"! Most cookers were made of iron with a cream vitreous enamel finish and a black or cream hob with large and small solid plates and a square, iron

grill/boiler. This was primarily the heating element for the grill but it was also used for slow cooking on the hob.

The grill chamber on the post war cookers usually had a drop-down door. Instead of standing on four short legs, the cookers were now being made in pressed sheet metal and were given a squared-off base, often with a warming drawer for plates below the oven.

The control knobs of the cookers continued to be placed at the front beside the oven – but there they were easily within the reach of small, inquisitive fingers. A better, safer place was to have all the controls on a raised panel behind the hob and this soon became the choice of all makers.

Some of the makers also added an automatic clock that would switch the oven on and off at pre-set times. Not all the early autotimers were easy to use: one owner awoke at 3.00 am on Christmas morning to smell his turkey cooked and ready for eating twelve hours too soon!

As man headed for the moon, that same technology was being used to change and improve both the kitchen and the cooker.

Pasta

ELECTRONIC OVEN CONTROL

Among many refinements and improvements of the 1960s was the grill chamber which became larger and could also become a second, small oven; the hob was given four fast radiant rings – some with dual circuits to suit small pans. After 1969 linings for the oven had a coating that resisted grease so never needed cleaning, and then came ovens with fan heaters which gave even heating throughout the chamber. These were British inventions or improvements on transatlantic ideas.

The designers were also questioning the basic shape of the cooker. Electricity had, up to now, been applied to shapes designed for other fuels. The 1970s saw the introduction of separate oven and boiling units – dividing oven and hob saved stooping, allowed more cooking space and the metal cabinet was replaced with a wood surround to make it more of a piece of furniture.

Opposite page:
A microwave cooker (Creda), modern slot-in cooker with ceramic hob (Creda), built-in oven and hob (Belling) and a tungsten halogen plate in use on a ceramic hob (Tricity).

The Victorians had tried hard to give their stoves "eye appeal" with decorative ironwork and beautifully constructed hinges that you can often see today – and not just in museums! The designers of the 70s strove, too, to link good appearance with function. One example was the ceramic hob that was first seen in 1966. An accidental discovery when a furnace went wrong in an American glassworks, this attractive, opalescent surface proved to be as strong as cast iron, but yet capable of conducting heat vertically through its surface. The electric heating elements mounted underneath needed no protective metal sheath, and, when switched on, just the patterned areas on the ceramic surface (which could serve also as a counter top) became hot. In 1982 came a new method of hob cooking using tungsten halogen lamps which give off heat similar to those used for lighting. Cooling is faster and more controllable. Further research has now produced a method of replacing the heating elements with a magnetic heat induction coil – a device which heats the contents of the pan rather than the pan itself.

Microwave cookers

Most dramatic development of all is the cooker that does not use direct heat at all but instead uses electro-magnetic energy – microwaves that are similar to radio waves. Although a magnetron which creates the microwaves had been designed

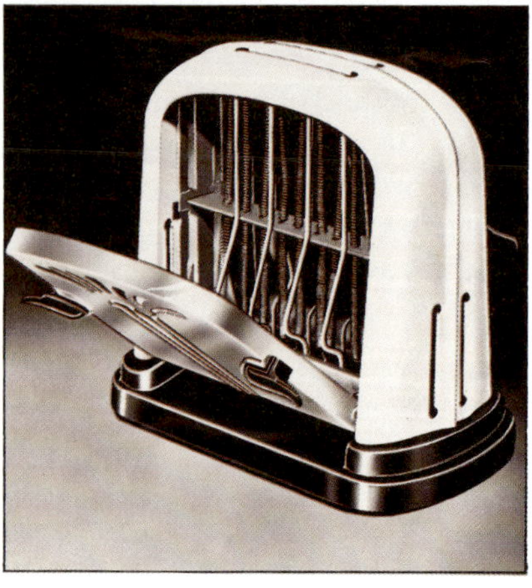

experimentally in 1924, it was two Englishmen, Dr. H.A. Boot and Sir John Randall who, in 1940, discovered and developed a high powered version which was to give Britain its war-winning lead in airborne radar. They discovered that water in the path of a microwave radar beam heats up. At first this was regarded as an irritating complication but, since food contains moisture, they realised that food placed in a metal box and subjected to microwaves heated up very rapidly indeed – in seconds rather than minutes.

The first microwave cooker for sale appeared in 1947 in the U.S. and it was not until almost ten years later that large commercial models were sold in the U.K. designed for the catering market. A small, domestic model was not designed until 1965 and a version arrived in Britain in 1972.

The microwave cooker has since proved so successful, because of its speed, its energy saving features and its compact size, that there are now many cooks who think that one day it might even replace the conventional cooker.

Opposite page top: Breakfast time in 1939 with electric food warmer, coffee pot and toaster. This early type of toaster reversed the bread when the side was opened. ***Below left:*** An alternative design (1938) had a sliding drawer. ***Right:*** A popular toaster of 1949 (HMV); – soon ousted by the pop-up toaster. The 1988 version (this page) has automatic browning.

The small cookers

Electricity made possible the use of small, portable cooking appliances. They could be used in any room with a socket outlet and it meant that some meals, like breakfast, and some dishes could be cooked away from the kitchen. Most were faster, more efficient and used less energy than the cooker. The electric toaster is faster than the toasting fork or the grill; the electric kettle more efficient than a kettle on a hob.

The first electric toaster was British – made by Crompton & Company in 1893 but the slices of bread had to be reversed by hand. Then came a model that ejected the slices from the end. The pop-up toaster was the invention in 1926 of an American whose first models had a tendency to launch the slices six feet into the air – frequently on fire! The double-sided toaster in the form now owned by thirty-four per cent of households in the U.K. dates from 1937, although it was not common in Britain until 1949.

The contact grill, two plates of heated metal placed in direct contact with the food and, known as an infra-red grill, was a British invention. It dates from 1922 and was revived in 1966 – serving as a sandwich toaster or a fast grill in today's improved version.

Another British invention that was ignored at first was the "kettle-cooker". This appeared in 1971 in the United States to revive and improve on the age-old method of tenderising meat and retaining flavour by cooking for many hours over a slow flame. The electric version does this better and more economically since the heat source and the food are enclosed together within one cooking pot.

Among other more portable cookers that applied the simplicity of the electric heating element to a conventional cooking task were the electric saucepan (1893); the frypan (1911); the deep fat fryer (1942) and the yoghurt maker (1969).

Modern electric frypan.

TURN OF THE WHEEL

Previous page:
"A maid of all work" was the advertising description of this 1914 vacuum cleaner.

One of the first suction devices for cleaning was operated by bellows attached to the housemaid's feet.

The development of smaller electric motors – this one 1880 – made possible many home appliances like the portable vacuum made by BVC in 1904 (right).

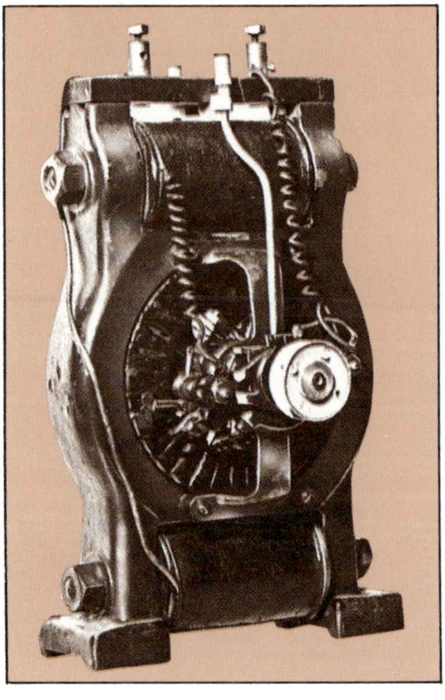

The story of the electric motor

In a power station generator, mechanical energy derived from steam, internal combustion engines or water power is used to rotate an electro-magnet inside coils of wire held in a stationary frame. As the magnet revolves, pulses of electric current are generated in the coils. This makes use of the principle discovered by Michael Faraday in 1831 that led to the use of electricity to provide power and light.

An electric motor uses the same kind of equipment to convert electrical energy into mechanical energy. By applying a current to the coil winding in a motor two magnetic fields are produced, one in the stationary frame and the other in the moving part. It is the interaction between these two magnetic fields that makes the moving part rotate very rapidly.

The electric motor is one of the most efficient of all energy converters – capable of transforming into work over 90 per cent of the energy that reaches it. The steam engine is only between 16 to 30 per cent efficient and the petrol engine in the car about 15 per cent.

Another Englishman, James Clerk Maxwell, studied Faraday's discoveries and he, in 1864, worked out in mathematical terms the fundamental theories of electricity and magnetism. These calculations enabled other scientists to design electric motors of all sizes and types, including those used in home appliances.

Electric fan

The first small, practical electric motor was designed by an American immigrant, Nicola Tesla in 1889 and its first home use was for a small table fan that sold so well that, in 1891, he produced a fan motor that could have its speed regulated.

Vacuum cleaner

The first use of an electric motor to simplify housework was in a floor sweeper. A cleaner that lifted dirt out of carpets, upholstery and curtains by suction had been invented by Cecil Booth in 1901. He called it "the vacuum cleaner". If you wanted your home cleaned a horse-drawn cart arrived at the door and the dust was extracted through pipes laid through the windows – the power being a petrol engine.

It was a cumbersome arrangement and, in the early days, the police summoned Booth for causing an obstruction. What was needed was something that could be used by the maidservants and numerous ingenious inventions appeared, using portable bellows. In one of these the bellows were strapped to the feet of the maid who, clutching a hose in her hands, walked about the room hopefully drawing in the dust and dirt.

These bellows cleaners were largely ineffective, except in redistributing the dust. What was required was more suction power and so in 1904 Booth produced a portable cleaner using an electric motor mounted on a trolley. It plugged into a light socket, but it was bulky and heavy although effective at collecting dust.

An American caretaker, J. Murray Spangler, heard of Booth's invention and, although he had not seen an illustration, he set about designing one for himself using his wife's broom handle and one of their pillowcases for a dust bag. Spangler, who was employed by the Hoover family, suffered badly from asthma and his objective was to find something to do his cleaning work for him so the dust would not aggravate his condition. Hoover was impressed with his solution and persuaded him to patent it in 1908.

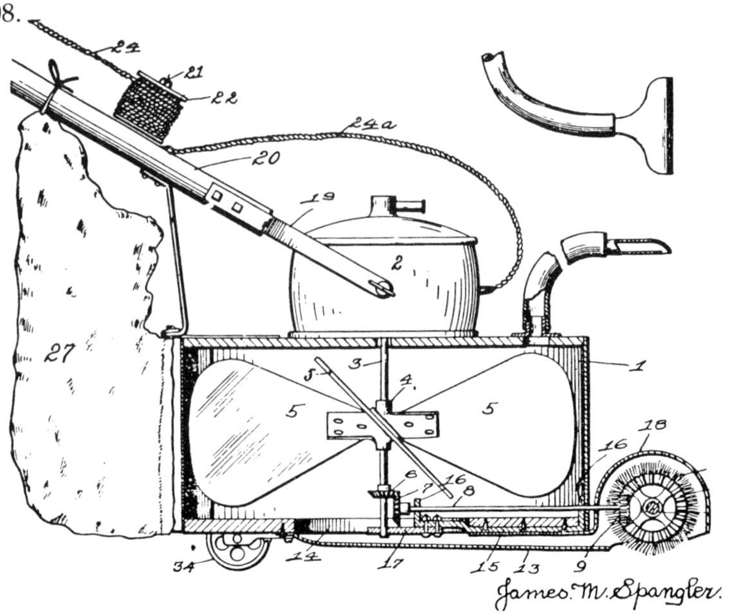

Spangler's US Patent 889 823 dated 2 June, 1908 led to the development of the popular 'bag and stick' cleaners. These are two early Hoover versions of 1909 and 1912.

HOOVER

Hoover, who was a saddle maker, converted part of his factory to make a few models of the "vacuum carpet sweeper". They sold so quickly that he devoted himself to the business – and so successfully that today the word "hoover", meaning to clean a carpet mechanically, is to be found in the dictionary. Spangler retired and lived comfortably on the royalties paid to him by Hoover.

The first Hoover arrived in Britain in 1912 and it cost £25 which was more than the annual wages of most of the maids who used

This 1906 vacuum cleaner, nicknamed 'the pram', competed with the hand operated models and the 'electric box' vacuum cleaner.

Opposite page: Vacuum cleaner of 1930 with its 1988 upright and cylinder successors.

Below: Goblin advertisement

it. Booth and his British Vacuum Cleaner Co. Ltd. had not been idle and he had improved on the first designs to produce a model which was cheaper.

By 1915 there were more than a dozen firms making "vacuum cleaners". Almost half a million homes had now been wired for electricity, all of them where servants were normally employed to do the housework, but with the recruiting for the armed forces or for the munitions factories a "mechanical servant" to do the dusting, and selling for about £7 became very popular.

There were also benefits to health. When a serious outbreak of Spotted Fever broke out amongst soldiers at Crystal Palace, vacuum cleaners were used to remove 23 tonnes of dust. The British Vacuum Cleaner Company reported "the health of the men improved immediately, when all conventional attempts to control the epidemic had failed".

In 1918 a Swedish firm called Lux (later named Electrolux) further improved on Booth's ideas and enclosed the motor and the fan in a metal cylinder. At one end was an outlet to which a long hose could be attached and to this was fitted a variety of shaped tools to suck in dust – not just from the floor, but furnishings, upholstery and curtains.

Hoover continued to develop the stick type of cleaner and by 1926 he had added a beater bar with brushes. This was driven by the motor to lift dust from the carpet so it could be sucked into the cleaner.

An upright cleaner was produced by Booth's company in 1921 and in 1926 they adopted the trade name "Goblin" for all their cleaners.

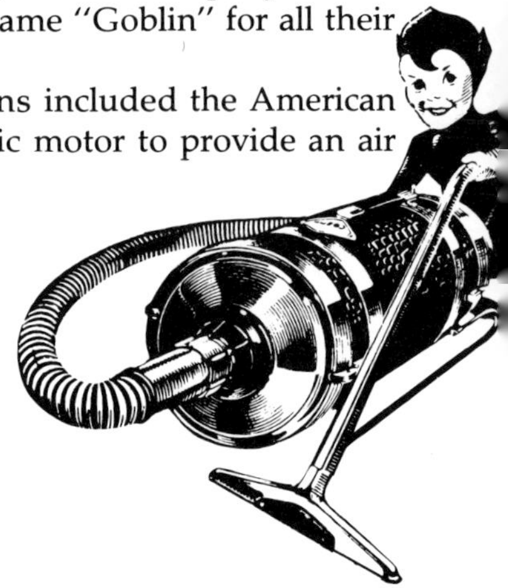

A variety of other ingenious designs included the American "Airway" which also used the electric motor to provide an air flow for a hair dryer. There was also a system that had outlets in every room leading to a large motor, fan and dust bag installed in a cupboard or in the cellar. By 1939 the popular selling cleaner was either the type where you pushed the motor ahead of you – the upright – or pulled it behind you –

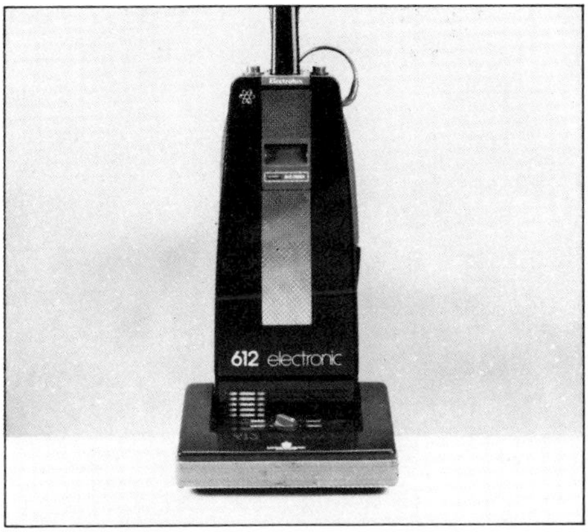
612 electronic

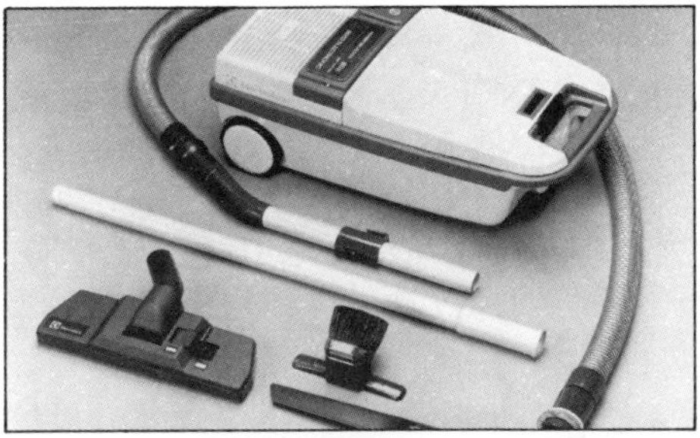

KENWOOD
UNIVERSAL
FOOD MIXER AND BEATER
MADE U.S.A.
1918

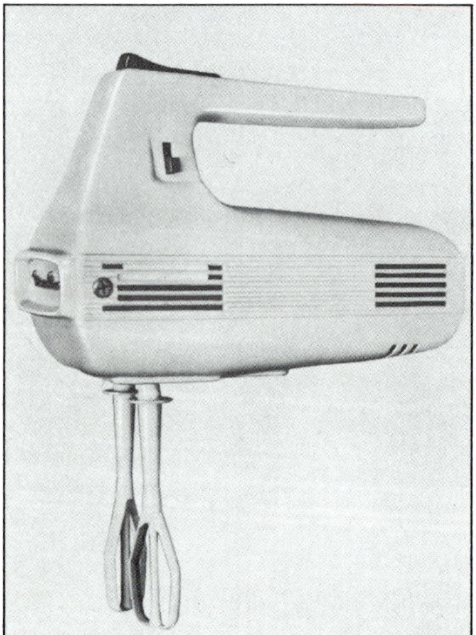

the cylinder.

In the post war period there were many improvements. Smaller, more powerful motors gave better suction power and one model, made spherical in shape, used the same principle as the hovercraft to aid movement along the floor.

Now to be found in more than 90 per cent of homes in Britain, the modern suction cleaner comes with a range of cleaning attachments for various purposes – essential for the cylinder model, but now supplied as an extra for the upright. Other features include power driven nozzles for the cylinder cleaners, flex winders, disposable dust bags and some models come with the motor mounted on the handle so they can serve as either cylinder or upright cleaners.

Opposite page: With its modern counterpart in the background, the 1918 food mixer shows an unchanged principle of motor driven beaters. *Below:* a 1944 design with a juice extractor attachment, and a lightweight hand held model of 1962.

Food mixers

Another popular application of the electric motor was in mixing and grinding foods but it was not until the development of compact, reliable electric motors in the 1930s that a variety of kitchen equipment came into use for mixing.

The first practical food mixer came from America in 1918. Its beaters extended into the bowl and mixed from above – a design that was unchanged until 1952 when a mixer was invented that had its motor in the base with the blades fitted into the bowl.

In the 1920s and 30s the electric motor was applied to all sorts of culinary tasks like mincing and shredding which later became attachments for some of the more powerful food mixers. Blender/liquidisers and can openers appeared in the mid 1930s in the U.S. and the electric slicing knife in 1939 where two serrated blades slid side by side, driven by a motor. This was an improvement on the circular slicer where the food being sliced was moved against the revolving blade.

Hand-operated bacon slicers were to be seen in every grocer's shop from the turn of the century and many of these were converted to electric motor power; a small domestic circular slicer appeared in Germany (for slicing sausages) in 1937.

J.W. Powers of the General Electric Company in America is credited with the invention of the food waste disposer that fitted into the sink outlet in 1929, although it did not go on sale until 1935. In Britain in the 1960s a version was developed that could also be used as a clothes washer, a vegetable and shoe cleaner and a food mixer, simply by connecting attachments to the motor.

Curiosities

Among the more curious motor powered ideas for the home that appeared in the 1930s was the automatic, motor driven "waker" which stripped the clothes off the bed when the electric alarm clock rang!

More sensible was the automatic bedside teamaker. This was invented in a practical form in 1904 by a Birmingham gunsmith, although his design was not electrical. An arm linked to an alarm clock struck a match which lighted a spirit stove which heated a kettle. When the kettle boiled it tilted and poured the water into the teapot and extinguished the flame. Mr. L.G. Hawkins of Drury Lane adapted the idea in 1920 and linked an electric clock with an electric kettle in a simple machine but the first popular machine to supply the now famous bedside "cuppa" was patented by Brenner Thornton in 1936 and sold by "Goblin" for £5.15s.6d.

Electric mousetraps, cockroach catchers and an astonishing collection of health, beauty and slimming aids appeared, albeit briefly, between 1910 and 1940. To read the publicity of the period, you would be led to believe that electricity was capable of curing most of the common ailments – from acne to lumbago. Many of the electrical gadgets were endorsed by eminent physicians – some were even invented by them. "A daily dose of electricity", wrote one enthusiast in 1922, recommending mild electric shocks, "is better than £100 of pills and potions".

One of the most successful and practical survivors among the motor powered appliances is the electric shaver. The first was designed by a retired American Army Officer, Lieut. Colonel Jacob Schick in 1928. This used the principle of a cutting surface sliding back and forth behind a shearing head. In Germany in 1933 a smaller version appeared

Philips Shaver 1947.

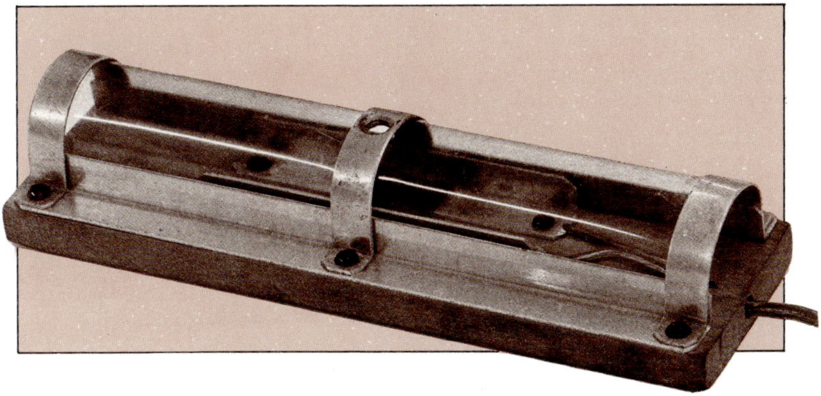

Electric shaving mug (1926), and a device for electrocuting mice (1926). These and many other electrical 'curiosities' are on display in The Milne Museum, Tonbridge, Kent.

that closely resembled the hand razor and used standard razor blades that had to be honed after each shave. A completely different approach was taken by Professor Horowitz of Philips in Holland in 1937. He designed a circular cutting head – the Philishave.

Along with the shaver came a very popular appliance – the electric shaving mug that heated its own water.

Power drills, power saws, sanders and the range of garden aids such as mowers, hedge trimmers and lawn rakers, all gradually emerged in the late 60s and early 70s as popular home appliances because of the better design of the alternating current motors – some of which were now able to run at different speeds and adjust themselves to cope with heavier loads.

Now we depend on motor power to run many of our central heating systems; even the mains drainage system and gas supply for the modern home is dependent on electricity. In industry, electricity is the life blood, and motor power its arms and legs.

A motor driven fan distributes thermostatically controlled warmth from this modern room heater.

COOL IT

The story of refrigerators and freezers

Keeping food fresh and free from the attention of vermin was an everyday problem for our ancestors. Food had to be carefully covered, or hung in crates or nets from hooks in the ceiling to keep it away from rats, mice and insects. Bigger homes had stone larders with stone shelves and, until this century, kitchens were traditionally painted blue – a colour which was supposed to keep away flies.

Previous page: Electric refrigerator 1935.

Opposite page: Ice house at Hatchlands (Surrey), a National Trust property. Dome and entrance roof would have been covered with a layer of earth to give extra insulation for the food stored in the underground chamber.

Keeping food cool prevented it from going "bad" – this was known centuries before there was an understanding of harmful bacteria. The Roman emperors had fast chariots that brought ice from the Alps, protected by thick sacks. The Romans were also credited with inventing the iced drink.

The ancient Greeks found that food kept fresh longer if stored in damp earthenware jars cooled by evaporation – a method still widely practised today in Third World countries.

Salting, pickling, smoking, and sun drying were – and still are – all methods of preserving foods but the results do not match storage at low temperatures.

From the end of the seventeenth century large country homes had ice houses built in their grounds for cool storage of perishable foods like meat and poultry. These were underground vaults lined with stone or cut into rock and the bottom half filled with ice collected in the winter from a nearby lake or pond and covered with a thick layer of straw. Well insulated from spring and summer temperatures, food kept cool for some time – the opposite of that other sensible idea where today we insulate the walls and roof of our home to keep in the warmth in winter!

The "ice box" – a hardwood, zinc lined cabinet usually insulated with felt – was the first refrigerator. It had to be constantly filled with fresh ice which until 1939 was sold from door to door from horse-drawn carts.

The ice was brought by boat from Norway, or by fast clipper ship from North America and Greenland, and, by the end of the last century, over half a million tons of ice a year in large blocks were being shipped into British ports.

As it was a difficult, heavy and very perishable cargo, efforts were made to find mechanical methods of refrigeration. It was already known that when certain liquids were evaporated they absorbed heat from their surroundings – in other words, cold was produced. Michael Faraday had noted this in 1823 when he was making a study of ammonia but just as with the electric motor, whose principle he discovered two years earlier, he was unable to see a practical application.

Fortunately, there were many who did see the possibilities, among them two Scotsmen who developed a chemical method of making ice by rapidly evaporating water and, in 1834, an American – Jacob Perkins – working in London, designed a compression/cooling machine which he sold to breweries and wholesale butchers.

James Harrison, a Scottish printer who had emigrated to Australia in 1837, became interested in Perkins' discovery along with the work of two Americans, John Gorrie and Alexander Twinning. Harrison, who had observed the cooling effect of

German zinc-lined refrigerator of 1880 needed daily ice placed in a central compartment. The tap provided iced water.

Opposite page: American ice box of 1895 took ice blocks in top left cupboard to provide cooling for the food.

ether, planned to make his fortune by shipping frozen meat to England but his method of refrigeration was mechanically unsound and the voyage in 1873 ended in failure. The entire rotting cargo had to be dumped at sea.

It was then the turn of a German schoolmaster, Carl Von Linde, who used compressed air to reduce the temperature in insulated compartments and, in 1880, the first cargo of refrigerated beef and mutton from Australia arrived in London, "in excellent fresh condition though it has been six months on the voyage".

The idea was so successful and "chilled, fresh meat" became so popular, that other versions were built for markets, warehouses, shops and hotels. Some of the refrigeration "compressors" were powered by steam but the arrival of electricity and the electric motor gave a more convenient power source – compact and reliable, needing little attention.

Railways, fast steamships, and a good road system meant there was a much wider choice of food available for storage in the new, large, commercial refrigerators. There were now many of the new food shops and markets which stayed open for twenty hours a day, seven days a week and, as there was no shortage of servants to collect and prepare the food, a refrigerator for the home was, at first, thought unnecessary.

It was not until 1913 that a domestic version was designed, powered by an electric motor. This was called the "Domelre" (domestic electric refrigerator) and was made in Chicago. A version of this "expensive novelty", which was also bulky and heavy, appeared in London in 1919, to the annoyance of a British company who had designed something similar in 1912 without finding anyone to take a serious interest. A French company copied the American idea and perpetuated the name "refrigerator" rather than "ice box". Several wealthy families purchased models when they appeared in 1921 mainly because it was "an excellent way of cooling champagne"!

Then in 1923 the American firm, Frigidaire, introduced their "electric ice box" to Britain. It was popular because it was less expensive and smaller than its predecessors. Even so, at about £60 – the price of a secondhand car – it was only for the comparatively wealthy.

Two young Swedish students, von Platen and Munters, while still at college in 1922, developed a different type of refrigerator. They wanted to make something simpler and cheaper than the American ice box and looked back to an idea of a Frenchman, Ferdinand Carré. Carré had demonstrated in London back in 1862 an ice-maker that worked by compressing ammonia using, not a mechanical method, but heat. He had called his method "absorption" and the two young inventors kept this name.

In the modern refrigerator a liquid with a low boiling point is evaporated and then reliquified. In the process of evaporation it

Left: A multi door refrigerator 1937 designed for the small shopkeeper.

Right: This Electrolux water cooled refrigerator of 1929 was in daily use until 1970.

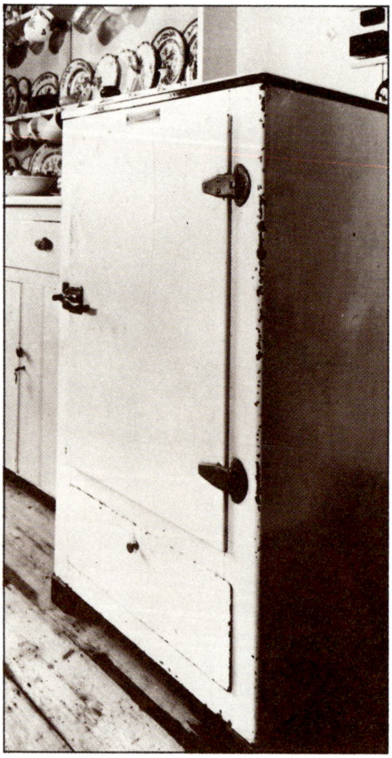

absorbs heat from its surroundings (the cabinet of the refrigerator) and when it condenses it gives up this heat. To make it evaporate it is compressed either by a motor (compressor) or a small electric heating element or gas flame which is the principle of the absorption models. In this evaporated state it is moved to the back of the refrigerator where it can expand to give up its heat. The liquid is then moved on to start the cycle all over again.

The absorption refrigerator has the advantage of being silent for it needs no mechanical parts to maintain the cycle. It is, though, slower than the compressor refrigerator and uses slightly more electricity.

The Electrolux Company bought the absorption idea from the two students and started to manufacture it in Britain in 1927. Their first models cost £48 and had a capacity of 10 cubic feet. The models had a cork lined wooden cabinet but they had to be

Kitchen of a London home 1937. A cast iron range has been replaced by an electric cooker and the family have a refrigerator with an ice making compartment, its motor compressor housed in the lower section.

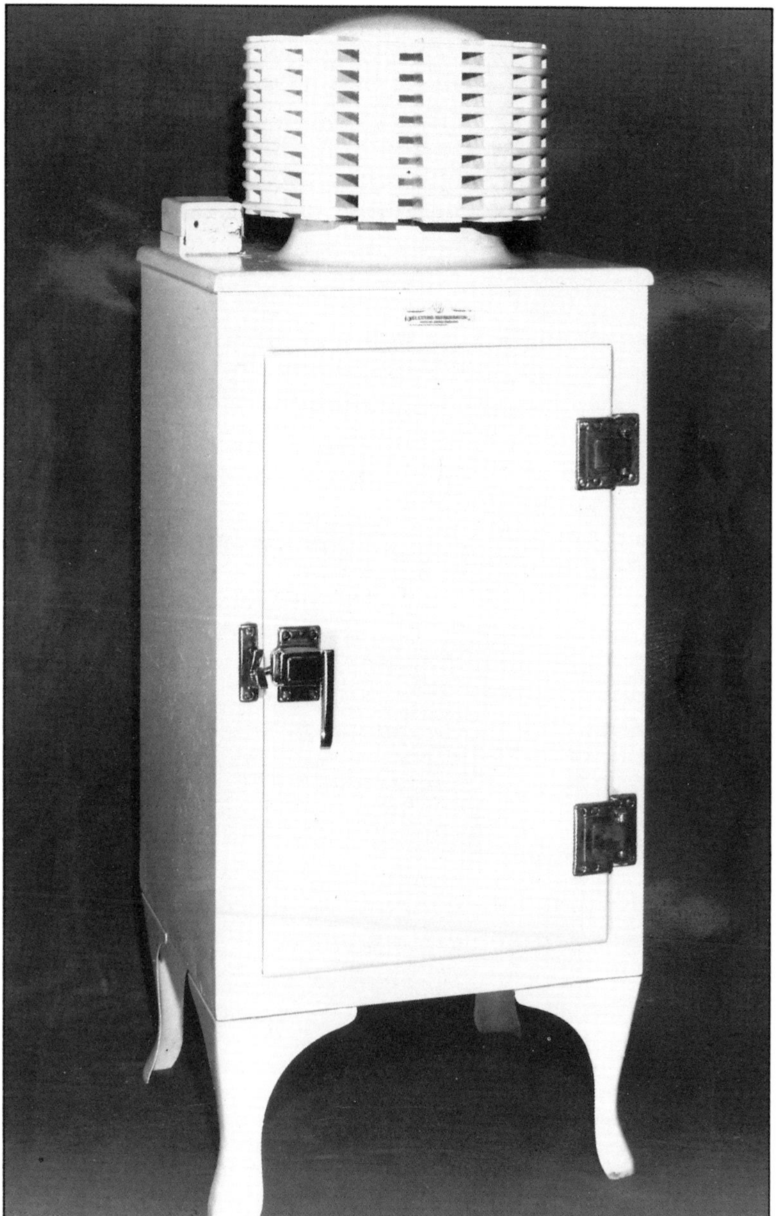

Popular 'beehive' refrigerator of the early 1930s. The unit with its cooling coil was conveniently mounted on the top but the refrigerant contained sulphur dioxide which, if it leaked, gave off a repugnant smell.

permanently connected to a cold water tap to encourage the refrigerant to give off the heat collected from the cabinet. In hot summer weather considerable quantities of water were needed to keep the cabinet cool and many water boards insisted on making a charge.

In 1932 Electrolux produced at their new Luton factory the first popular domestic model that did not need cold water. It had a steel cabinet and had only one cubic foot capacity – "sufficient", said the advert at the time, "for six pints of milk and two pounds of butter." It cost £19.15s. or "six pennies a week on easy terms".

It was still a slow start for refrigerators, even though – in 1927 – the Food Preservatives Act limited the use of dangerous, chemical artificial preservers so that essential perishable foods had a short life and became more expensive. Then in 1934 there was a very hot summer, a phenomenon to be repeated in 1959, and in both years the sales of refrigerators boomed.

By 1939 200,000 homes had a refrigerator; in 1960 it was five million; today it is over sixteen million.

Except for a few small models designed for caravan use, most of the modern electric refrigerators are now of the compressor type. The refrigerant is dichlor-difluoro-methane – almost as difficult to say as it is to spell – so it is known as "R12". All are much more compact than the early models. They have a frozen food compartment for low temperature storage (between −8°C and −18°C compared with the 7°C constant in the cabinet); are less bulky, using an insulation of expanded plastics, and many have push-button or automatic defrosting.

The food freezer

Because food destroying bacteria will not readily multiply at low temperatures, freezing food and storing it at −18°C is the most natural way of preserving it. This idea, it seems, occurred to Francis Bacon, the Elizabethan philosopher and scholar. It is reported that he died from a chill in 1626, caught after trying to freeze freshly killed chickens by stuffing them with snow.

The American inventor and explorer, Clarence Birdseye, while on a hunting trip in Labrador in 1923, noticed that fresh meat and fish exposed to the arctic temperatures tasted perfectly fresh when thawed and cooked months later. He spent the next seven years developing a freezing process where cartons of perishable food were placed between refrigerator plates and in 1930 he began to sell frozen vegetables over the counter to the public – a new industry had begun.

The packets were designed to be taken from the shop which had a freezer and be eaten the same day, although homes with a refrigerator were able to store them for a day or two. Nobody realised it at the time but, as refrigeration and food freezing became more popular, they had no need to shop as often and they were able to go further to larger shopping centres. This was to reduce dependence on the small corner shop and be a factor in the development of chain stores and supermarkets.

The refrigerator and the food freezer also had a marked effect on our choice of foods. The consumption of fresh foods and dairy products increased (with benefits to our health) and the consumption of salted and dried foods declined.

After 1959, refrigerators specially designed with compartments for the storage of packets of frozen foods appeared. Earlier models had only a small evaporator shelf designed mainly for making ice cubes in trays.

Soon there were refrigerators with a choice of one of three different types of frozen food storage compartments – for one week's safe storage, or one month, or three months. Almost at the same time (1950) the food freezer for the home arrived. This was called a "Deep Freezer" after the name of the company that first marketed them extensively in the U.S.A., and most were versions of the food conservator cabinets designed for shops, hotels and restaurants.

Few of these early "Deep Freezers" were able to maintain temperature low enough to freeze fresh food. It was not until 1955 that food freezers were sold for the home, capable of maintaining −18°C, and able to get down to −20°C and below when needed. They appeared first in the U.S.A. and then in Britain from the following year.

The first food freezers were large chests with lift-up lids but by 1961 small front-opening models came on to the market, including a matching pair – refrigerator and freezer – that could be built into a kitchen. These were first shown in London in 1961 and the next year English Electric introduced the "Fresh 'n

A modern cabinet that combines an automatic defrosting refrigerator mounted above a food freezer (Tricity).

Freeze" – a combined, front-opening refrigerator and freezer.

The refrigerator and the freezer have today replaced the walk-in, ventilated larder that used to be the only means of storing perishable food in the home. The prediction is that the home of the future will have a combined, three-temperature cabinet for food storage. First section would be a refrigerator for the perishables like milk and butter; a second section would be a food freezer for longer term storage; third, a cool cupboard for fresh vegetables, fruits, bread, cake and for cooling drinks.

There is even a possibility of reviving an invention introduced experimentally in a few homes in 1954; a cold storage cupboard where the heat drawn out is utilised to warm the household water supply.

A larder 'heat pump' designed to supply hot water and refrigeration 1954 (Ferranti)

SOAP AND WATER

The story of home laundry

Previous page: Washing machine with power wringer 1930.

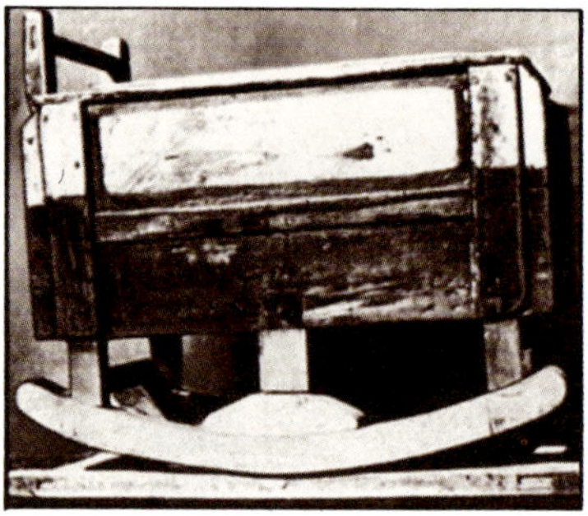

Rocker clothes washer 1862 (Tickenhall Collection, Bewdley).

Before about the middle of the last century clothes were washed only if it became absolutely necessary. Water was a precious commodity that had to be carried quite a distance in buckets. Few homes had a piped supply and soap was an expensive luxury heavily taxed until 1853 when a cholera epidemic made the Government realise the importance of encouraging cleanliness and hygiene.

Until that date most homes made their own form of soap. Tallow (mutton fat) was mixed with wood ash (apple tree ash was said to give the whitest wash) and this was rubbed on the clothes soaking in a tub of water. In the country the clothes could be washed and rubbed using smooth stones at the shallow edge of a river or stream. It was not a frequent practice and a clergyman in the Scottish lowlands in 1882 found the smell in his church so offensive that he demanded his congregation "improve upon the practice of cleansing their church clothes the once a year at Easter".

Few homes had a kitchen. Washing was done in a sink in a room built off the living room, called a scullery and, after about 1847, those that could afford it had a piped water supply. Some sculleries had a brick hearth for heating a cauldron or copper of water; some of those better off financially built a separate wash house or they made use of a commercial laundry that collected and delivered weekly. These laundries opened in just about every town and city from 1860; some even operated in country areas, usually run by a family working from home. The poor could make use of a municipal wash-house, a service that was started in Liverpool by Kitty Wilkinson, a poor but public-spirited washerwoman, and by 1870 had spread to most cities and large towns.

Using a wash tub and lots of hot water, the servants – or sometimes a laundry woman hired for the day – rubbed the

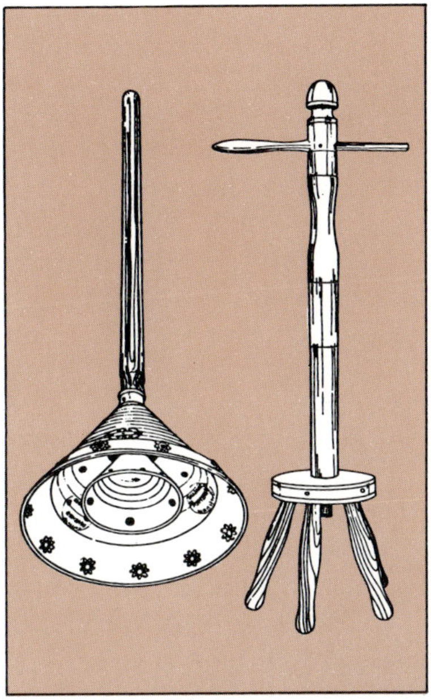

Left: The posser and the dolly, washing tools of the 18th century.

Right: A mechanical washer made by Thomas Bradford & Co 1857.

Home laundry in the 19th century. The woman on the right is making 'lye' a common substitute for soap.

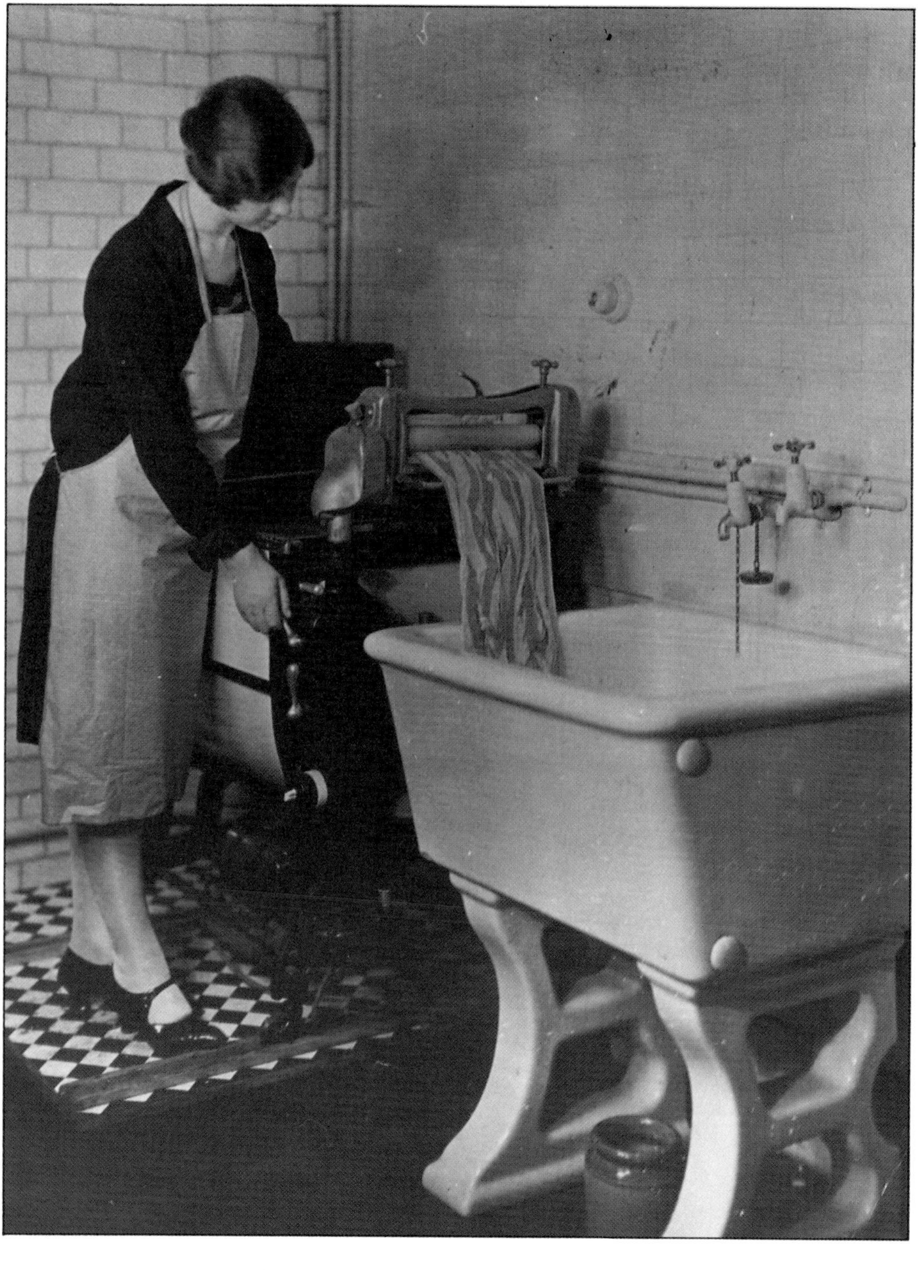

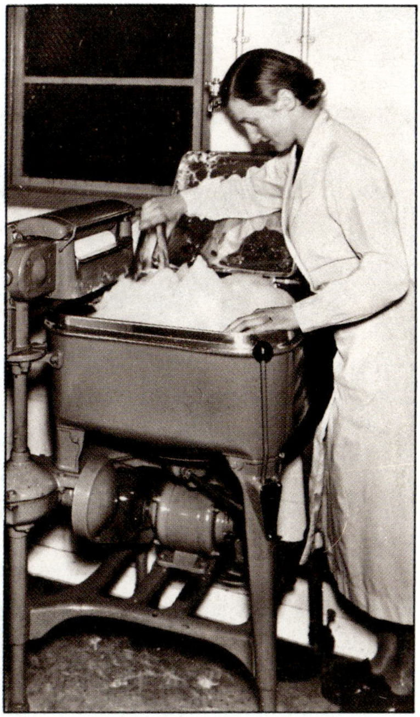

Washing machines of the late 1920s.

clothes against a washboard that had a corrugated surface made of wood, glass or metal within a two-legged wooden frame. The clothes were first pounded and stirred with a "dolly" or a "posser", to loosen the dirt. The "dolly" had a pole with a T handle at one end and, commonly, a three-legged wooden stool at the other. The "posser" or "posher" was a pole with a conical end of perforated copper.

The first washing machines were made in about 1810 and had a dolly that was rotated by a handle like a butter churn. As this was found to tangle the clothes, the first practical machines dating from 1845 had a set of cog wheels fitted so, as the handle was turned, the clothes moved first in one direction and then in the other, anticipating the reversing action of most of today's machines.

All these washing machines had casings made of wood and, instead of a reversing dolly, some of them had a wooden board that pressed up and down on the clothes; others were shaped like a pram and had a rocking action.

After washing, the clothes were rinsed and then the water was squeezed out, usually by hand, sometimes between two boards. In 1859 the roller wringer made its appearance and was described as "the marvel of the age" for the water was quickly pressed out by passing the clothes between the wooden rollers. In 1865 a Frenchman designed a revolving barrel with perforated holes to remove the water by centrifugal action. The invention was admired and even adopted by some commercial laundries, but it could not compete with the popular "mangle" and the idea was almost forgotten. It was to be almost seventy years before the domestic "spin dryer" came into its own and ousted its rival.

In 1908 a young American engineer, John Fisher, attached a small electric motor to a machine which, through long driving belts (to keep the motor away from the water) made a dolly revolve back and forth. It was not really a success but Fisher and other inventors persisted and, by 1916, they discovered that by putting the dolly at the bottom of the washtub and sealing in the motor, it was not only more efficient but safer to use. With this method the clothes – not the water – were pushed to and fro and the dirt came out easily. This was the *agitator* – the washing action later to be used by all single and twin-tub machines.

An alternative method developed for some machines had a revolving cylinder within a wooden drum – the first of the *tumble action* machines common today.

Combined washing machine and spindryer made by Savage in the USA in 1924.

Opposite page: First of the compact, British made washing machines with a hand wringer made in 1948 and sold for £31.5s.

By 1934 both agitator and tumble action machines were being mass-produced in North America within cabinets of white enamelled iron and steel rather than wood (which had to be hand-built). Two firms also remembered the idea of the Frenchman and, as early as 1924, offered a spin dryer as an alternative to the wringer.

All these machines were large, cumbersome, expensive and very heavy, so only comparatively few appeared in

Hoover

Great Britain. The British housewives preferred to use a laundry, a local wash house or an electric "wash boiler" such as the Burco, mounted on adjustable legs. This had a drain-off tap and a five-foot flexible cord with a splash-guard to protect contact points. It cost about £6.10s. (£6.50p).

The war interrupted development and sales. When it was over and the engineering factories switched from munitions to peacetime production, they looked at the pre-war wash boiler and decided it needed modernising. They based their new designs on an idea of George Gibson – another American. First Hoover and then Burco in 1947 produced a machine with a variation on the agitator – a propeller-like disc called an impellor, which was set in the side of the tub to stir the water. These machines were fitted first with a hand-wringer on the top and – in 1953 – a power wringer.

Three years later came the revival of a better idea – the spin dryer – and almost overnight wringing clothes was dismissed as old-fashioned and inefficient.

The next year – 1957 – saw the revival of another idea when Hoover introduced a spin dryer fitted into the same cabinet as the washing machine.

This new "twin tub" was a considerable improvement on the 1937 American design. The washing drum was not much bigger than the spin dryer; the smaller size being made possible by another remarkable invention – powder detergent. Soap on its own had never been very efficient for washing clothes. A lot of very hot water was needed to maintain a lather and then remove the suds. Powder detergents, derived from oil, did not need boiling water – indeed, compared with soap, they did not need much water at all to get the clothes clean.

Since the housewife had become used to seeing foam and lather, a little soap was simply added for effect but now the makers thought she was ready for a machine that worked best if it did not have to push a lot of water around. There was also a need for a machine to cope with the new man-made fibres like nylon, that could be harmed if washed in very hot water.

Machines that combined washtub and spin dryer together began to appear in the 1950s, first in the coin-operated, do-it-yourself laundries that opened in towns and cities

A 1956 housewife using her spindryer; her 1988 counterpart washes and dries her laundry in two automatic machines (Creda).

throughout the U.K. Although it was not realised at the time, these front-opening automatics were to decide the choice and shape of future washing machines for the home.

In 1956 vertical drum, agitator machines were introduced by Thor, Parnell and Hotpoint but other firms – like English Electric and Hoover – put their engineering skills into producing machines with the drum on its side where loading of the clothes was carried out from the front, like the "coin-op" washing machines. The advantage was that the clothes were then tumbled through the water instead of the other way around but, because this meant using less water, the detergent needed to be one of the type that made almost no lather. The machine could also be programmed to supply automatically the right amount of water at the right temperature, give a correct number of rinses and the right spin speed and time to suit the different fabrics.

Those who had used the "coin-op" had found that washing could be dried completely after spinning, using hot air drawn in or blown through the clothes in the drum. A domestic version of the tumble dryer was introduced by Parnell in 1958 although both Bendix and Thor had introduced in 1957 a washing machine that could tumble dry as well as wash and spin in the same drum. These first combined machines were not always reliable but, by 1978, improved mechanics and micro-technology started to be used and spin speed increased; controls were more accurate and washing performance improved.

Dishwashers

The dishwasher had a similar history to the washing machine – indeed, in 1946, one manufacturer introduced a dual machine with two tubs – one for clothes, one for dishes. The first dishwasher was shown in New York in 1910 but no practical model came on sale until 1932, and in Britain in 1937. Compared with other major appliances it has been rather slow to gain popular acceptance despite the fact that the average daily time taken at the sink, without a dishwasher, is 68 minutes.

In 1962 in Seattle a new form of dishwasher was shown by Kelvinator – one that used neither soap nor water. Cleaning dishes was carried out by sound waves – ultrasonics – but development since has been halted. Now, with the need to

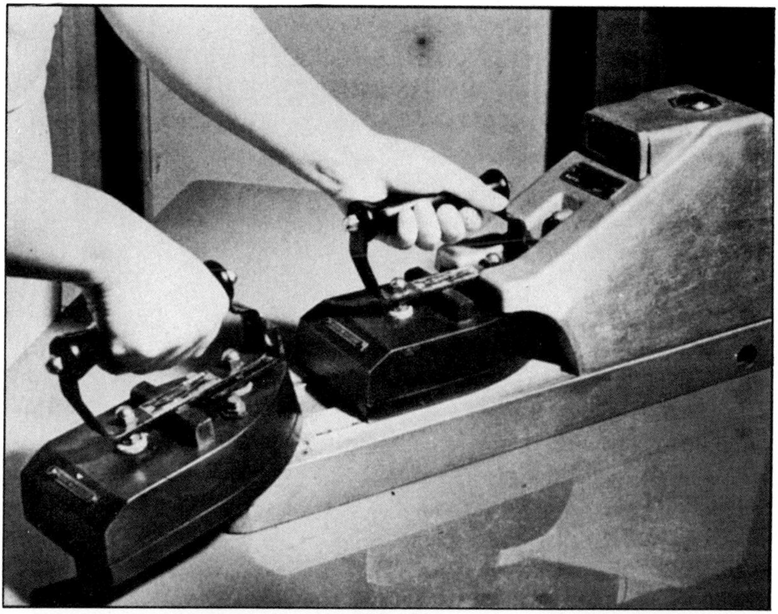

Above:
Cordless electric iron first invented in 1883.

Below:
Promethus iron of 1904.

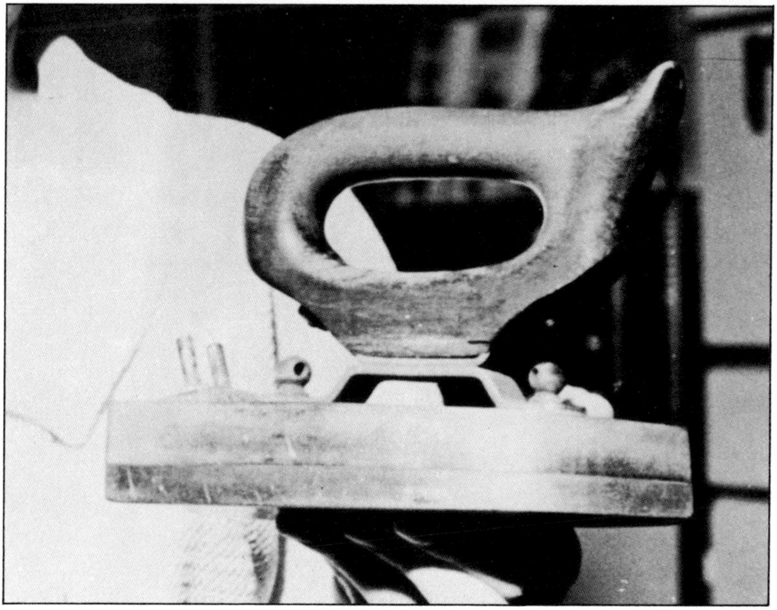

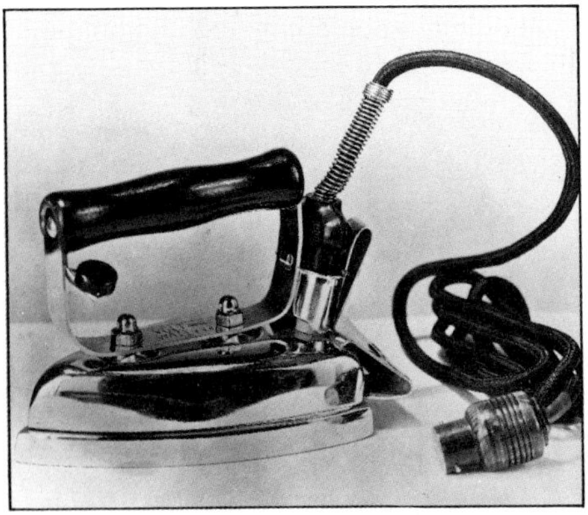

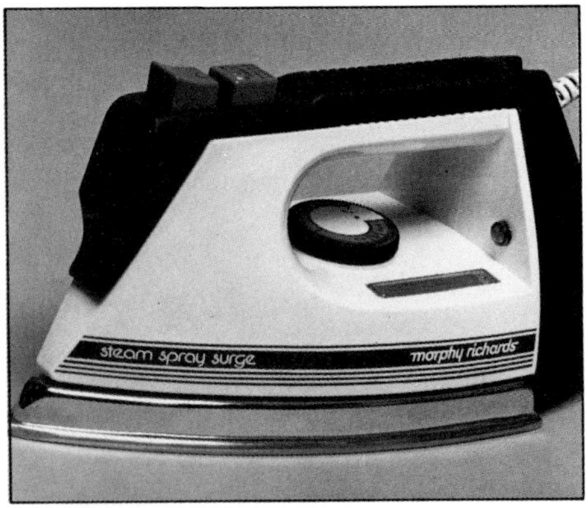
steam spray surge
morphy richards

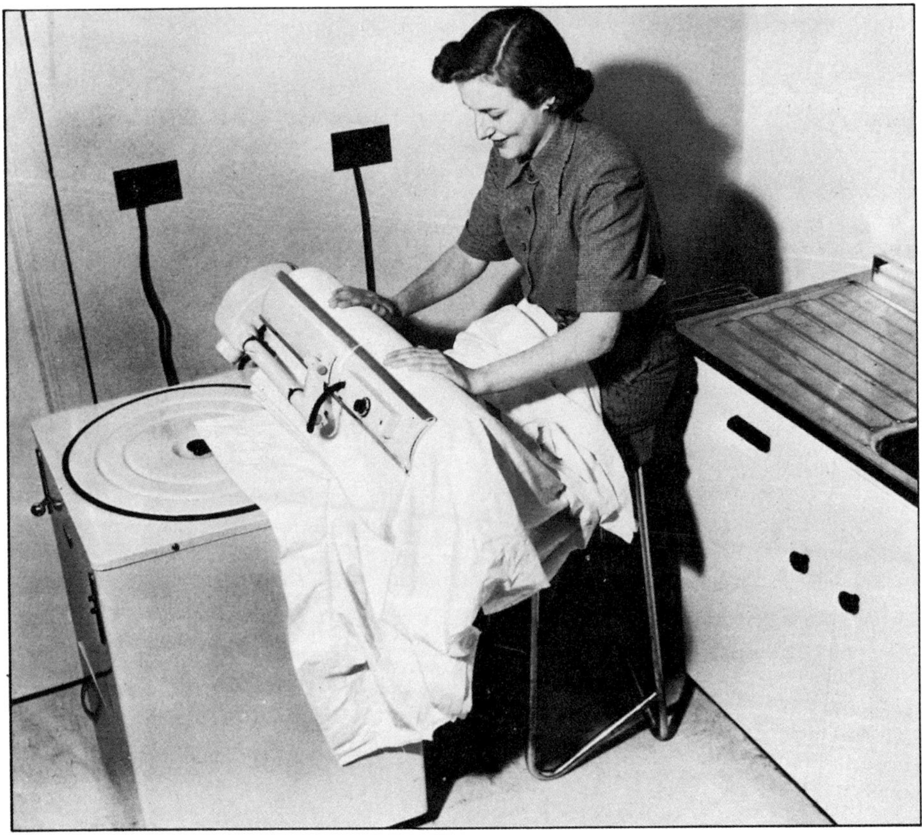

conserve energy, the idea may be revived and there is even talk of a version that will clean clothes as well. One difficulty though with cleaning by sound waves is that it may be necessary to develop special crockery and fabrics.

Ironing

Opposite page.
Top: Electric iron designed for connection to a light socket (1930) and a modern steam iron (1988)

Below: Washing machine with rotary iron (1950).

It was not just drying the clothes that was a problem but getting them smooth and shiny. Heavy, smooth stones, heated near a hearth and pushed over the clothes removed washing creases. Then came the "iron" – a block of thick metal with a handle. Beeswax or candle grease was used to make the heated surface slide over the linen and all kinds and shapes of iron were used from Elizabethan times (they were even mentioned in Shakespeare's plays) until well into this century.

Clothes finished with a hand iron were known as "laundry" – the rest was just "washing". In the Victorian era ironing was considered a particular domestic skill and in 1888 Mrs Beeton – the renowned author on domestic management – described a range of irons of different sizes according to the work for which they were intended. Some irons were hollow and were filled with hot embers or charcoal; some were made specially for ironing lace and delicate petticoats.

In larger households in the last century table and bed linen was smoothed and finished in a linen press consisting of a frame and stand with the top crossbar supporting a wooden screw. This screw then pushed down a wooden board on to the folded linen. Or there was a mangle – similar to the clothes wringer but with smoother rollers.

The first electric iron appeared in France in 1880 but it used an electric arc to create heat and pieces of red hot carbon were often shed on to the clothes burning little holes!

In 1883 a cordless electric iron was designed and patented by two engineers, Dyer and Seeley, in America. This had a special stand in which the iron was placed and plugged to heat up, but it was expensive and unreliable and was shown off more as a curio.

More practical irons were demonstrated in London, New York and Berlin in 1890 (one had been made in 1889 but it unfortunately exploded, killing its inventor).

Both the GEC and Crompton Companies in 1891 were selling irons with the sole plate heated by an electric element and a flexible cord connecting it to a lighting point or socket outlet.

Although the basic design of the electric iron had now been established, it was not until 1920, when a growing number of homes had an electricity supply, that a popular priced model was on sale in London. This iron cost eighteen shillings (90p), weighed 9lb (4kg) but there was no heat control to regulate the temperature.

The first iron with a thermostat arrived in 1936. It had a choice of 5 temperatures and the electrical loading was 500W or 1000W, priced about thirty-two shillings (£1.60p).

In 1963 Hoover introduced the steam-or-dry iron in Great Britain. This produced jets of steam to dampen dry clothes for pressing or ironing. In 1967 came a version that was able to spray a fine mist of water. Other improvements in the following years have included standardised temperature settings for the iron to match the care labels on garments, button slots, a water gauge, smoother sole plates and interchangeable right-hand, left-hand flexes.

Successful efforts were made, too, to mechanise the whole ironing process using electric heating. The tailor's press and the padded heated rotary iron of the commercial laundry were scaled down in size to fit the home. That they never proved widely popular was mainly due to parallel advances in fibre technology. The number of garments that needed ironing had been gradually reduced to well within the capabilities of the modern electric iron which can do the average week's ironing for a family in less than two hours at a cost of less than 5p.

In 1898 a Victorian housewife in Liverpool recorded in her household accounts book that her family laundry sent out for the week had cost three shillings and twopence. She had also paid a laundry woman sixpence; there was twopence for ironing and twopence-farthing for soap and "blue" (whitener). Converted into the value of today's money she was paying more than her modern counterpart with her fully automatic machine and modern iron that takes a fraction of the time.

WARMTH WITHOUT WASTE

526

ELECTRICAL DEPARTMENT

Electric Heaters in a Variety of Styles and Sizes

Electric Heaters require no attention, give off no fumes or smoke, and are instantly available at any time of the day or night

EL 521 PORTABLE MAGNET HEATER
A Pedestal Bowl Fire by means of which warmth can be radiated in any desired direction. This heater can be used on a lighting circuit. Current consumption 600 watts .. 21/-
Large size 30/-

EL 524 MAGNET SHEET METAL FIRE
In Black and Real Bronze finish
2,000 watt size .. £2 3 0
3,000 watt size .. £2 18 0

EL 523 ART METAL MAGNET FIRE
Made in two sizes
2,000 watts .. £4 0 0
3,000 watts .. £5 5 0

EL 526 PREMIER BOWL FIRE
Well designed cast base, with solid Copper reflector. Excellent heater. Consumption 600 watts
11 ins. dia. Bowl .. 18/9
12½ ins. dia. Bowl .. 27/-

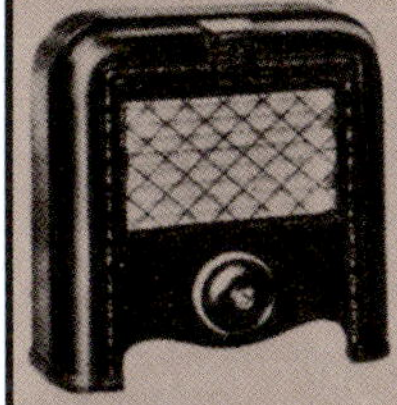

EL 522 ORNAMENTAL CAST IRON FIRE
Finished in Black stove enamel, or in vitreous Enamel. Brown, Green, Grey and White. One element controlled by a switch. Mounted on the front of the fire. Consumption 1,000/1,500 watts per hour .. 39/-

PLEASE STATE VOLTAGE WHEN ORDERING

Harrods Heaters are each supplied with two yards of heating flex

EL 5 HARRODS 'MAGICOAL FIRE'
Jacobean design. Antique bright finish (rustless). Size over all 20 ins. wide × 28 ins. high × 16 ins. deep £16 0 0
Maximum consumption 3 units per hour. Controlled by 3-way switch

EL 26 HARRODS 'MAGICOAL SUNBEAM FIRE'
Bright rustless finish. A realistic effect of flames and smoke give a delightfully cheerful atmosphere
Maximum consumption 3 units per hour with 3-way control
Size 16 ins. wide × 26 ins. high × 13 ins. deep £10 0 0
Size 19½ ins. wide × 26 ins. high × 13 ins. deep £13 0 0

EL 525 MAGNET REFLECTOR FIRE
Handsome design constructed in ornamental sheet metal and finished in Real Bronze or Oxidized Silver
Real Bronze finish
2,000 watts .. £9 5 0 3,000 watts .. £10 5 0
Oxidized Silver
2,000 watts .. £10 10 0 3,000 watts .. £11 15 0

EL 450 HARRODS 'MAGICOAL FIRE'
Just like a real blazing coal fire, but the heat of the 'Magicoal Fire' can be regulated by a turn of the switch
Brass and Bright Rustless Finish
£5 15 0
(Max. consumption 3 units per hour)
Special finishes to order
Prices on Application

ALL PRICES ARE SUBJECT TO MARKET FLUCTUATIONS

HARRODS LTD — *Telephone* SLOANE 1234 — *Telegrams* 'EVERYTHING HARRODS LONDON' — LONDON S W 1

The story of electric heating

Electricity was at first regarded as a reliable source of good light, simple to use, and with no smells and no need of regular maintenance. Yet, as miraculous as it seemed in the 1880s, and a big improvement on all other forms of lighting, it was admitted that the electric filament lamp was inefficient; far more of the energy used was converted into heat than produced light.

If, of course, you wanted a portable heater that needed no fuelling, and gave off no smoke, then the filament lamp seemed to be ideal! Mr H.J. Dowsing in 1896 designed just such a "heating lamp" with a frosted glass envelope. It had a 250 Watt carbon filament that gave off no light except the warm red glow. The Cannon bulb fire in 1904 had four of the "Dowsing Sausages" set against a polished reflector and controlled by brass switches.

The Dowsing lamp heaters were the first practical electric radiant heaters. The Crompton "electric fires" that were being sold in 1889 for £3 each were made up of resistance wires embedded into squares of cast iron, but they proved slow to heat up and cool down and they also went rusty rather quickly.

Previous page: Electric heaters in Harrods 1929 catalogue.

Left to right: Electric fires of 1912: a Dowsing lamp heater; the first Belling electric fire that could be adapted to boil a kettle and make toast, and a Ferranti radiant/convector heater (1919).

It was an apprentice at Crompton's firm who saw the disadvantages – and also the possibilities – and he started his own business in 1912 with the intention of making improved electric heaters. His name was Charles Richard Belling and the company he founded exists today where he started it in Enfield, Middlesex.

Belling had the idea of winding resistance wire on the front face of a strip of fireclay "which meant the wire was working at a red temperature in free air and heat from it was thrown forward". Belling used a new metal "Nichrome" which did not rust when heated. His heater was an improvement not only on Crompton's ideas, but on another invention called a Bastian heater. This had a resistance wire wound inside a quartz tube. It gave off a good heat but was not only expensive to manufacture but rather fragile.

Belling's first heater appeared in 1912 and was fitted with a trivet for boiling a kettle and with a warning "this fire is warmed by electricity so do not use a poker".

Simple electric fires with fireclay elements were developed by Belling and other firms until, by 1920, there were many kinds of "reflector fires" on sale. One mail order catalogue in 1929 listed

sixty-one different models.

The "fuel effect" fire was the invention of an Englishman, Mr H.H. Berry, who, in 1920 – lying in bed recovering from flu – became irritated by the housemaid constantly coming into the sickroom to make up the coal fire. He designed imitation coal and used the heat rising from a red lamp to revolve a slotted aluminium wheel to give a flickering effect.

Left to right:
Belling fan heater in veneered wood case (1937).
Popular fuel effect fires by English Electric (1924) and Belling (1921).
A small portable electric fire in a ceramic surround (1930).

A later development, in the 30s, returned to the idea of the Bastian heater. Instead of sitting inside a fireclay frame, the resistance wire was now protected inside a silica glass rod. This is now the most popular and most efficient type of heating element in use in electric fires.

Convector heaters with concealed heating elements warming air that passes over them were a parallel development.

The first appeared in 1910 but, as there was no reassuring red glow, they were not popular. Then, in the winter of 1914, the War Office ordered thousands to provide heating for the recruits "to fight the Kaiser". Radiant heaters and stoves were found to be too dangerous for the hurriedly built wooden barracks but the small convectors were safe and easy to instal.

The disadvantage was that convector heaters were rather slow and bulky. Robert Gordon in 1929 had the idea of placing an

electric fan at the base to speed air flow and reduce the size but nobody else saw the possibilities and there was no money to back his invention.

Then in 1937 Belling fitted a fan at the back of one of their convectors and, although it was effective, it was noisy. What was needed was a small, quiet fan and this was not found until 1953 when Bruno Eck of Cologne made a lightweight tubular fan powered by a small motor and placed behind the heating element. Within five years the compact little heater became the most popular type of electric heater sold anywhere in the world.

Electricity is very versatile: other forms of heating extend from tiny tubular heaters for heating an airing cupboard and dating from 1900 to the very slim panel heaters and the oil filled radiators. Another form – dating from 1959 – is ceiling heating where the elements are hidden out of sight behind the ceiling surface.

Storage heating

Because electricity had at first been used solely for lighting, the generating plant was idle for the greater part of each day. The electricity companies needed a continuous demand for electricity if they were to show a profit and they began a quest for "load".

Crompton's heaters from his first catalogue.

Heating more than cooking seemed the most promising as except for open fires, no public building had any form of heating. Electric radiators in ornate cast iron cases were designed with the heating elements embedded between layers of enamel on a cast iron base and they were advertised at prices from £6.

One such installation, carried out by Crompton and Co in 1895, was the Vaudeville Theatre in London. The winter that year was exceptionally cold (the Thames was blocked by ice-floes in February) and the theatre needed a system that could be installed quickly. Crompton and Co received the order at 11.00 am one morning and by 6.00 pm the same day the theatre was being warmed electrically!

As well as establishing Crompton's reputation for speed and efficiency, this success stimulated sales. Electric radiators were easy to install and no chimney was needed. It was also found that some materials retained heat better than others and this heat continued to be given out long after the electricity had been switched off.

One of the most successful heat storage materials was soapstone (magnesium silicate or stearite). It was incredibly heavy but soapstone did not split when elements were inserted and it was comparatively cheap. In 1904 the description of "electric storage heater" was used for the first time and small soapstone heaters, without elaborate cases, began to be sold for home heating.

Electricity has to be used when it is generated. Except in batteries it cannot be conveniently stored and, as industry turned to electricity, the need for continuous "load" for the generators moved gradually from the day to the night time. After 1947 and nationalisation, new electric power stations were being built, including the first nuclear stations, and electric storage heating was seen as an ideal means of providing this load. The term "off peak" was used to refer to hours in the early afternoon and at

Soapstone storage radiator (1930) with its modern slimline counterpart (Storad).

night when demand for electricity fell off and a reduced charge (tariff) was introduced to encourage the greater use of electricity just between those hours.

Not only soapstone but concrete, brick, sand, some chemicals and even water, were all found to be capable of retaining heat – especially when contained within an insulated case. By 1960 there were over forty different designs of storage heater, including one that combined an electric radiant fire.

Floorwarming systems with heating elements buried in concrete utilised the same thermal principle and were found to be a very effective form of central heating. It was first used to heat air-raid shelters in World War II but came into wide use when the supply industry offered "off peak" electricity at substantially lower prices. Unfortunately, some of the earliest systems dating from 1951 lacked a proper knowledge of insulation and an excellent system of heating had a shaky start.

The lack of thought in design showed up in some applications like the high rise blocks of local authority housing and these failures overshadowed its more numerous successes. Among many invaluable applications were heated roadways, such as The Mound in Edinburgh, to prevent winter accidents due to the frost, and under the stones of Salisbury Cathedral so there were no unsightly heating pipes and radiators to detract from the historic fabric which electric underfloor warming protects from damp and condensation.

In the post-war period, off-peak heating through storage heaters offered a system of home heating that was cheaper and easier to instal than many other home heating systems. The first rather bulky "Unit Plan" heaters dating from 1957 were gradually replaced until today the slim, insulated and controllable versions offer a clean, efficient method of home heating.

Electric water heating

The discovery that water was easily and quickly heated by electricity led to the development of electric water heaters – some as early as 1890. An electric geyser was developed in 1912 that provided boiling water at the rate of 12 pints a minute. It was smaller and more compact than anything else available at the time and cost £14. "There was just one snag", said its inventor,

Electric water heating at the sink (1930).

Charles Belling, "it took a 10kW load which in those days dimmed the lights for miles around".

It was not long before practical electrical water heaters appeared – the simple immersion heater that fitted into a hot tank in 1920. These were fitted with thermostatic controls that switched off automatically when the correct temperature was reached. Although dual immersions for sink or bath and special models for hard water areas have improved the efficiency and performance, the very successful designs introduced by Bray, Backer and Hotpoint in 1932 have remained substantially unchanged over the years and this type of immersion element is used today in 63 per cent of homes in the U.K.

Electric kettles were first designed with the heating element beneath the base. ***Right:*** 1914 kettle from Simplex. ***Left:*** 1922 model by Bulpitts who were the first to immerse the element in the water.

Electric bedwarmer (1920) designed to take the place of the hot water bottle.

Electric kettle

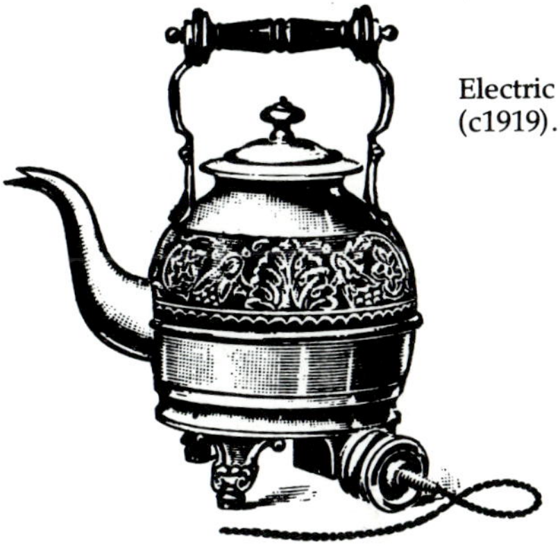

Electric kettle (c1919).

Simplest of all the water heaters is the electric kettle. This first appeared in Chicago in 1894, and in Britain in 1902, and is now to be found in more than three-quarters of the homes in Britain.

The kettle that switches itself off on boiling dates from 1955 although whistles, buzzers and flashing lights had all been tried prior to this to show when the water had boiled. A protection device to prevent the kettle being switched on if no water was present was another improvement of the 50s but the design has altered little except that the 1902 model took twelve minutes to boil one pint of water and the 1981 model will do it in 96 seconds – easily the fastest and most economical method of making a hot "cuppa".

Curiously, although it no longer needs to stand on a circular ring or flame since the heating element is immersed in the water, the electric kettle has still kept the traditional, circular kettle shape. "Kettles" that can be mounted on the wall so the teapot or pan goes to the heater rather than the other way around date from 1917 but only now are they coming into wider use.

Electric blankets

The passage of electricity through a resistor creates heat. This is the principle of all electric heating and an American, Sidney Russell, discovered in 1912 that a gentle heat could be obtained from an insulated length of metal tape laid inside two layers of blanket. He designed his heating pad so patients at his clinic who were suffering from chest ailments could sleep outdoors! Neither he nor his patients presumably realised the risk of electrocution. In 1937 one of his patients designed a blanket version which was advertised as "a night warmer for invalids".

In 1926 in Britain the Ex-Services Mental Welfare Society started making electric heating pads as they were a simple sewing job for the patient members. They used a German design whose inventors may not have been pleased to learn, after war broke out, that RAF maintenance staff adopted their idea for an electric blanket to keep night fighter aircraft engines from freezing up in winter.

The Society used the name "Thermega" for their pads and also a "multi-pad" version which they sold as a small electric underblanket in 1930. Thermega are also credited with the first use of an insulated resistance wire which they placed in flying suits, designed to provide warmth for air crew at high altitudes, and at a safe low voltage – 24 volts.

The first of the post war blankets were made with asbestos insulated resistors but they were only safe if they were kept dry. If the asbestos became wet there was risk of a shock and there were a number of fatalities.

All kinds of "extra safe" electric bedwarmers were then tried, including one introduced in 1970 by Thermega, which had an electric heater that circulated hot water through flexible plastic piping forming a grid sewn into the blanket. There was also the electrically heated mattress and a bed heater made by Belling from left-over parts of a wartime incendiary bomb "snuffer".

Another post war "adaptation" was the Yarworth Jones Bed Heater. In this, electric heating wires were fitted between a lightweight, plastic sheeting. This sheeting had been originally designed for the Mosquito fighter-bomber to provide protection against flak and the bed heater was believed to be bullet-proof!

A monitoring system to detect overheating in blankets was introduced by Dreamland in 1967 and, today, all electric underblankets and all-night overblankets contain safety devices and are manufactured to stringent safety standards laid down by the British Electrotechnical Approvals Board (BEAB) and carry the British Standards Number 3456 A4. They are perfectly safe when used in accordance with the manufacturer's instructions and have become one of electricity's most valuable and inexpensive contributions to modern living.

SOUND AND VISION

The story of home entertainment

Just over a century ago all sound was live – and as fleeting as the echo. Now sound can be stored on records or tapes and played back at any time or anywhere, thanks to electricity.

Previous page: Father and daughter enjoying television on a 14in set 1955.

The idea that pressure waves heard as sounds could form patterns occurred to an Irishman, F.L. Scott, living in France in 1857, and he invented a machine he called a *phonautograph*. Mr Scott's machine recorded sounds as scratches on a disc, and it impressed a Frenchman, Charles Clos, who then found a means of playing back the scratches on a machine he called the *paleophone*.

The year was 1877 and, in America, Thomas Edison had already constructed a *phonograph* (from the Greek words for "sound and writer") and he reproduced the first recorded message: "Mary had a little lamb" on a tinfoil cylinder.

Although it was regarded as a miracle, a major drawback was the fact that the cylinder had to be turned by hand. It was difficult to keep it at an even speed so the sound reproduced varied from low rumblings to high pitched squeaks.

Even when Chichester Bell (cousin of Alexander Bell who invented the telephone) patented the *graphophone* in 1886, which substituted wax for tinfoil, the *Musical Times* reported that all that was heard was "grinding from the interior sounds supposed to be a reproduction of most sweet voices".

Then a German, Emil Berliner in 1889, remembered Scott and Clos' idea and designed a disc rather than a cylinder and devised a needle that scored spiral grooves. Sound vibrations were recorded by the needle moving from side to side rather than up and down.

Berliner also invented the method of producing copies of the discs in a shellac/wax mixture from an original. Curiously, though, he saw his idea for the *gramophone* as having no future – except for the construction of talking dolls!

Edison, too, had a limited view of his invention. He saw its principal use as a dictating machine. It was the public, much to his annoyance, who decided to use it for pleasure, recording their favourite songs and performers.

Left to right: Edison's original phonograph (1877); an early horn gramophone (1906) and Berliner's gramophone (1889).

Radio

Edison was more interested in a patent by an Italian, Guglielmo Marconi, for *wireless telegraphy,* taken out in 1896, and one in 1900 which laid the foundations for modern radio reception by explaining how to tune a receiver to a selected transmission. A year later, in 1901, Marconi was to transmit signals from Cornwall to Newfoundland and *"radio-telegraphy"*, or *radio*, for short, had been born.

Radio waves are just part of a vast range of similar types of waves known as the electro-magnetic spectrum. Wherever you are reading this now you are surrounded by radio waves from countless millions of sources (transmitters), some of them far out in the universe; others from a local radio station. Some of these waves carry pictures as well as sound and most of the inventions in this chapter are for collecting, controlling and interpreting them, making them serve our needs for transmitting information and entertainment.

The gramophone became popular as soon as a clockwork spring motor had been developed to turn the discs at a constant speed. Radio was rather slower in gaining popular appeal as loudspeaker models required electricity and, although on 14th November 1922, the British Broadcasting Company started a regular broadcasting service, there were still more than three-quarters of the homes in Britain without an electricity supply. Accumulators (lead acid batteries) in glass containers that could be recharged at the corner shop for a few pennies allowed many to listen to the popular broadcasts but the method was inconvenient and the batteries unreliable. Popular journals carried advertisements from firms willing to do wiring: "No more batteries, electricity for a radio wall plug and electric lighting for your house – £20 or 2s.6d. a week" read one.

By 1930 radio sets had improved from a simple "crystal set" with a long, outside aerial and a pair of earphones, to a receiver capable of picking up radio signals over long distances and all contained inside a piece of furniture that could stand on a table. This was due to the invention and development of the radio valve by an Englishman, an Austrian and an American. Valves looked rather like light bulbs but were designed to pass electric current only one way and step up the power of the radio signal. Ambrose

Left: A five valve radio by Kolster Brandes Ltd of Sidcup, Kent (1935).

Right: Ecko Radio designed by J K White with a plastic case (1931).

Listening to the radio (1934).

Fleming, Robert von Lieben and Lee Forest, all working independently, perfected these valves – the basis of the *amplifier* which led to the production of mains radio.

Today, valves have been replaced by transistors, invented in 1948, and there have been many other technical advances so that the modern "radio" (now usually called a tuner/amplifier, or a receiver or a "tranni" – transistor) is not only smaller and much lighter but needs only a very small amount of electric current to make it work.

The same electrical principles that made radio a success were applied to recording. Instead of the clumsy method of scratching sound waves on wax, new electrical techniques enabled microphones to convert sound into electrical current which could be etched as "patterns" in the wax. In 1925 the first hit of the electrical recording era appeared – 900 voices singing the hymn, "Adeste Fideles – Come All Ye Faithful"!

The first gramophone discs turned at 72 revolutions a minute (rpm) and played for two minutes, but "Adeste Fideles" played at 78 rpm and lasted four minutes. In 1948 came the long playing record which squeezed up to a thousand grooves on a side and, playing at $33\frac{1}{3}$ rpm., produced a full half hour of sound.

The sound quality, too, had improved with the development of *stereo*. Since the listener listened with two ears it was thought the best way to reproduce sound was to record it with two "ears" and experiments and trials went on in the Bell Telephone Laboratories in America throughout the 1930s. The first stereophonic disc was patented by Electrical and Musical Industries in 1930, although it was to be a quarter of a century before it appeared in a popular form. The first stereophonic sound film track was used for Walt Disney's cartoon film "Fantasia" in 1941.

The principle of popular stereo is that separate microphone systems pick up and record slightly different strands of the same sound so that the reproduced sounds can be played back from discs by a "stylus" (instead of a needle) capable of vibrating in two directions at once, re-creating the conditions of the original recording.

Tape recording

In 1899 a Danish engineer, Valdemar Poulsen, had the idea of recording sound waves on steel tape. He called his system the *Telegraphone* as it was intended to be used to record telephone messages. The tape kept breaking and so the method was largely ignored until 1932 when Poulsen and a group of Germans each found a method of recording electrical impulses as magnetic patterns on a coated plastic tape. A British invention of this period achieved similar results with recorded speech using fine wire but it needed the arrival of electronic amplifiers and plastic tape before it was a practical invention.

Cassette tapes, smaller and more compact than the reel-to-reel type, arrived in 1953 and have now virtually taken over the popular market, even threatening the future of discs.

Television

Having captured sound reproduction, it remained only to find a means of capturing and transmitting visual signals. The cinema had achieved this with film at the beginning of the century and electricity's contribution was to improve the projected image using tiny light sources and also to add sound.

This was not enough for some inventors who remembered research carried out by an Englishman in 1873. Using an element called selenium, Willoughby Smith had shown that patterns of light could be converted into electric current and passed along a wire to be reproduced in the same form at the other end, using pieces of the same metal.

No application was found for this discovery until a number of inventors in the first quarter of the century tried to use it to transmit pictures, at first with the object of sending newspaper photographs long distances. At this they eventually succeeded, but moving pictures were a problem. Several systems were invented but the best proved to be an electron beam scanning a fluorescent screen from side to side and from top to bottom so fast that its movement registered on the eye as a single image.

The first demonstration of a television system was in 1923 by a Scotsman, John Logie Baird. Using a lamp, a perforated disc and

Stereo sound and television pictures from a disc is made possible using laser technology (Philips).

40p worth of equipment in a tiny loft in Hastings, Baird succeeded in transmitting moving pictures and sounds but, beset by chronic ill health, it took him until 1927 to develop his invention. Then in 1929 an experimental television service using his system was started by the BBC. A famous TV broadcast was the Derby in 1931.

There were still many technical problems with the Baird designs and in 1935 a committee of inquiry selected an electron beam system that incorporated Baird's ideas. This system, which used 405 lines instead of 240 lines, was produced by a talented EMI research group led by Isaac Shoenberg. They made a number of improvements including a high vacuum cathode ray tube for the receiver.

The first receivers cost £126 and the picture size measured only 14in (diagonal). The first black and white programmes were news broadcasts and Walt Disney cartoons with an occasional concert and sometimes a film.

It took almost ten years of further research after the war ended to produce a practical TV set and a national TV service. Sales of sets were boosted by the Coronation in 1953 which was televised live. By 1955, 17in pictures were possible and, the following year,

Though the size of the screen on this 1937 television was only twelve inches, the tube was so long that it had to be mounted vertically and viewed through a mirror in the lid.

a TV receiver with a 23in picture was available.

Research was also going on into presenting colour pictures, developing an idea of Baird's where the basic signal wave was divided into three – one for each of the primary colours. The first sets sold in America in 1954 had problems in keeping the colours in balance and, by 1956 – when the first experimental colour transmissions were tried out by the BBC – they used a system called Phase Alternation Line (PAL for short) with 624 lines. Although based on the American National Television System Committee's (NTSC) method, PAL was able to give better colour reproduction and it was adopted by all other countries, except for France, Russia and their satellites who developed a method of their own called SECAM.

Video recording

Baird had made the first video recording – on disc – in 1928 but the first video tape recorders, developed by Alexander Pontiatoff, a Russian-born engineer working in America, did not arrive until 1956.

Home video tapes – a development of the magnetic sound tapes – arrived in Britain in 1972 and these machines can even record a programme from one channel while you are watching another on the screen. You can record TV programmes while you are away from home and it is even possible to make your own TV programmes using a small, portable TV camera and recorder.

The video disc (1977) is the latest development. You cannot use discs to record from your TV but films, concerts and sports events are sold in the same way as long playing records. Possibly, with the stereo sound now proposed for the TV set, these video discs may replace the gramophone disc that began it all to give everyone not only "the Sound of Music" but the sight as well!

Nor does the story of TV end there. A library of current information can now be provided from the TV set – the Teletext system, started in 1973. The BBC version of Teletext is called Ceefax and it gives on the screen news and up-to-date information in words and figures. Soon it may be possible to transmit personal visual messages on to the screen, using one of the variations of Teletext and, as well as checking on current prices at the supermarket, you should even be able to order goods from your armchair.

Electronic games and educational puzzles, first seen in 1975, are also making use of the TV set. The TV screen can even be used to display information stored in a computer which can be programmed to operate controls in the home such as heating or can remind you of appointments – its messages appearing even while you are watching a TV programme.

The future

What further changes will come about in the next one hundred years as a result of the application of electricity to mankind's service? Human achievement is based on man's ideas and the fascinating thing about all discoveries and inventions is that we can see how one idea in the mind of one individual at one moment in history can change the course of civilisation. The process is continuous because every discovery and invention is developed by others and, in turn, this inspires further invention.

This, then, is only the beginning. Tomorrow's world will be as different as ours is today when compared with that of a Britain which enjoyed its first public supply of electricity that autumn evening in 1881.